Unsui

A Diary of Zen Monastic Life

Unsui:
A Diary of Zen Monastic Life

drawings by *Giei Satō*

text by Eshin Nishimura

edited and with introduction by Bardwell L. Smith

 An East-West Center Book
The University Press of Hawaii
Honolulu

Contents

Foreword

Since Buddhism began in India about twenty-five centuries ago with the Buddha Shākyamuni, it has undergone development in a number of countries, each of which has contributed the influence of its particular culture. Buddhism as a whole, however, can be regarded as having two different aspects: one is "true awareness," which is Buddha's own religious experience, at the core of his teaching; the other is composed of Buddha's teachings themselves, over a forty-nine year period of his life. Needless to say, these two aspects cannot be separated, for they are united in the personality of Buddha.

The history of Buddhism has nevertheless produced a number of sects and schools which arose out of an emphasis upon one or another of the Buddhist scriptures. Typically, the Zen sect of Buddhism has maintained that the existence of sects and the dependence upon scripture separate man from the essence of Buddhism — that is, true awareness. Zen Buddhism finds its own special significance in bringing man back to the center of the Buddhism that is Buddha's religious experience, while at the same time holding all of Buddha's teachings in respect, as being the expression of that original experience.

Today, another approach to Zen in the Orient regards Zen as the source of all possible religious thought, as pointing to the existence of true being beyond all dualism. In this sense, Zen is seen as the ground out of which all religious thought is freely combined and given its inner vitality. When one views Zen in this light, one may have Confucian Zen or Christian Zen. Of course, while such a position is possible from a Zen standpoint, one might expect criticism from other points of view. At any rate,

Zen sees its uniqueness in its efforts to transcend denominational distinctions. This is perhaps the principal reason for the sympathetic understanding of Zen shown by Japanese intellectuals, who feel that Zen has a special significance in helping man to create a higher culture.

To turn now to the history of Zen Buddhism: it originated in China in A.D. 520, when Bodhidharma (called Daruma in Japan), the twenty-ninth Patriarch of Mahāyāna Buddhism, came to China from India, and declared the importance of true awareness, as distinguished from merely studying or lecturing about Buddhist scriptures. Zen Buddhism (in Chinese, Ch'an) developed under the influence of the practical Chinese mind. For about seven hundred years, during the T'ang and Sung dynasties, Chinese Zen Buddhism enjoyed a period of brilliance. In the thirteenth century great Zen masters — both Chinese and Japanese — brought it to Japan, where it flourished in a new cultural climate.

Japanese Zen Buddhism, over the course of its development, produced two characteristically different currents. One is the Sōtō sect, which teaches the oneness of zazen* practice and satori awareness; the other is the Rinzai sect, which emphasizes satori experience through the hard discipline of kōan exercise. Among the various schools of Rinzai Zen, only that of Hakuin Zenji† (1685-1768) survives today. Zen Master Hakuin established the so-called kōan method (Kanna Zen) to bring the student to the great experience of satori awareness, and was also instrumental in regulating monastic life in its present form. At the same time, Hakuin showed his great compassion toward the

* Words appearing in color on first use may be found in the Glossary.

† Japanese personal names are given in Western order; that is, with surnames last. (The apparent exception is Hakuin Zenji: Zenji is not a name but a title that customarily follows the surname.)

common people through his preaching, his Zen paintings, and especially his writing, which was readily intelligible to the ordinary reader—unusual for Buddhist works of that period.

This traditional Hakuin Zen school was first introduced to the United States by Zen Master Sōen Shaku, Abbot of Engakuji in Kamakura, when he lectured on Zen Buddhism at the International Congress of World Religions, held in Chicago in 1893. Shortly thereafter, the young D. T. Suzuki was sent to America by his own Zen Master, Sōen Shaku. Suzuki devoted his long life to the introduction of Oriental thought, primarily Zen Buddhism, to the West, drawing upon his deep wisdom of Zen experience and his vast knowledge of philosophy. The principal motivation of my several visits to the United States has been to follow that precious devotion of D. T. Suzuki.

It seems to me, from my impressions of these last ten years, that the West's interest in Zen is moving from mere curiosity to a more sincere understanding, from an intellectual approach to a practical one. It is unquestionably difficult, however, to transplant into an entirely different environment a religion or philosophy evolved over a long period in a country with its own distinctive culture and traditions. The problems of language alone are immense.

In this sense, therefore, the present volume, with its illustrations revealing the severe discipline of Zen training touched with a warm and gracious humor, may prove especially significant, by providing Western readers with a realistic introduction to Zen monastic life. The Reverend Eshin Nishimura, who comments upon each drawing, is a former monk of my monastery. Because of his firsthand knowledge of the West combined with his personal experience of Zen, he is one of the few persons qualified to interpret Zen monastic training adequately. Since his comments

have been written with a Western audience in mind, I hope
that this book will start the reader on the direct path to
satori awareness.

Zenkei Shibayama
Abbot of Nanzenji
Kyōto

Preface

To My Friends in the West

During January 1969 I participated in a seminar on Buddhist meditation at Oberlin College to help students in their understanding of Zen Buddhist practice. Later, in 1970 and 1971, I spent ten weeks at Carleton College, giving one course on the history of Zen Buddhism, and another providing instruction in zazen. Through these courses, and many discussions with students of several colleges and institutes in the United States, I have come to realize that people in the West are increasingly turning their attention from mere intellectual or theoretical interest in Zen Buddhism toward its actual practice. In my meetings with a great number and variety of Zen meditation groups all over the country, I have been made aware, by their sincerity in practicing Zen meditation, that Zen Buddhism no longer remains an exclusively Oriental treasure.

It was marvelously fortunate, in this sense, that I brought with me on this tour ninety-seven paintings of Rinzai Zen monastic life. They were drawn by the late Zen priest the Reverend Giei Satō, who died on November 30, 1967, at the age of forty-seven. He was not a Zen Master, but an ordinary Rinzai Zen temple priest who loved to draw pictures for the children of his neighborhood, as a way of illustrating for them the teachings of Buddhism. What comforted him most during his last years was his memories of his youthful days at a Zen monastery. He expressed these recollections in pictures, so that his Zen spirit might live on after his passing. I am sure these pictures were drawn for no one besides himself. The reader may be astonished to see humor expressed here, considering that they were sketched by a man facing death. There are no feelings of sorrow, however, only brightness and joy in both figures and color.

Zen monastic life has not been revealed in this fashion to the public before, as monks dislike being disturbed by visitors whose interest may be only superficial. While some photographs of Zen monastic life exist, they do not catch its flavor, nor its total regimen and rhythm of life. Notice the faces of these monks. Can such expressions be captured in a photograph?

In the middle of February 1969 I visited Pendle Hill, the Society of Friends' center for religious study and practice near Philadelphia, where I had spent a year during 1960 and 1961, and was asked by friends there to show slides of these pictures. I was then urged to have these pictures published for people throughout the English-speaking world. The Institute for Zen Studies (located at Hanazono College, a Rinzai Zen institution in Kyōto) where I am a member of the faculty, accepted this offer with great pleasure and permitted me to write a commentary based on my own personal experience for each picture. The originals of these pictures are kept at the Institute.

Finally, I would like to express my gratitude to three persons: Barry Jackman of Carleton College for his editorial assistance and his preparation of the Glossary of Japanese terms; Bardwell Smith, also of Carleton College, for his editing of the manuscript, his helpful Introduction, and his making possible the publication of this volume; and Zenkei Shibayama, Abbot of Nanzenji, for his Preface in this instance — but above all, for his example as a Zen Master.

Eshin Nishimura

Introduction

In 1934 there appeared for the first time in a Western language a work describing the life in and regimen of a Zen Buddhist monastery. This work, the *Training of the Zen Buddhist Monk*, by D.T. Suzuki, was then, and remains so even after its author's death in 1966, the most widely read interpretation of Zen outside Japan. A facsimile edition of the original volume, to which Professor Suzuki added a new Introduction, was published in 1965.[1] An important part of both editions of this work was the illustrations contributed by the Rinzai Zen priest Zenchū Satō, described by Suzuki as "not a professional painter, but being one of those who have gone through all the disciplinary measures pertaining to the Zendō life, he is thoroughly imbued with its spirit, and what he has depicted here is the record of his own experience."[2]

The present volume, coming nearly four decades after Suzuki's book first appeared, arrives at a time when there is considerably more known about Zen Buddhism by Westerners than in 1934, though very little of the literature available in English has concerned itself with what has always been the practical working heart of Zen: the daily life of the Zen monastery.[3] The accent of the present volume, while

---

1. Daisetz Teitaro Suzuki, *The Training of the Zen Buddhist Monk* (New York: University Books, 1965). The original edition was published in Kyōto by The Eastern Buddhist Society in 1934.

2. Ibid., p. xxviii.

3. One exception to this is an essay by Gary Snyder entitled "Spring Sesshin at Shoko-ku-ji" in his volume *Earth House Hold* (New York: New Directions Publishing Corporation, 1957), pp. 44-53. As Snyder says in this essay, the term Unsui (literally "cloud, water") is from an old Chinese verse, "to drift like clouds and flow like water." Another constructive series of essays may be found in *Secrets of the Lotus: Studies in Buddhist Meditation*, ed. Donald K. Swearer (New York: The Macmillan Co., 1971), pp. 129-211. These pages include an essay by Eshin Nishimura on Zen training; a translation by him of the Zazen-gi [On zazen meditation], a T'ang dynasty meditation manual on the rules for contemplation while sitting, as

it supplements that of Suzuki's, is considerably different. Suzuki's emphasis was more upon the life and training of the monk as told by the author than upon the illustrations by Zenchū Satō;[4] in this volume, it is just the reverse, the pictures speak largely for themselves.

The illustrations appearing here, however, were done by Giei Satō, more than thirty years after those in the Suzuki volume. Though there is a similarity of motif and scene, the present work contains more than twice the number of illustrations and presents them in the colors of the drawings themselves, not in black and white. Just as important, the illustrations are arranged in a sequence broken only by the brief comments of Eshin Nishimura, who provides suggestive detail without impeding one's appreciation of the drawings themselves. While the present arrangement is inevitably arbitrary to a degree, there is a certain logic to the sequence which becomes apparent as it is studied.

It goes without saying that the present text, both commentary and introduction, makes no pretense of being scholarly in a technical sense. It is designed for a broad readership, though, because of the general unfamiliarity of the subject itself, it is hoped that even those teaching in various fields of Asian culture may find it of interest and value in their work. As with the arrangement of the illustrations, so the selection of themes upon which to comment here is somewhat arbitrary. Even the decision to include an introduction that focused attention upon various themes was not made without weighing the pros and cons. In part, the decision was based upon the fact that Suzuki had subdivided his treatment of

---

well as six lectures on this text by Mumon Yamada Roshi; and finally, a chapter on Hakuin Zenji's eighteenth century exposition of the Prajñāpāramitā Hṛdaya Sūtra [The heart of the perfection of wisdom], also translated by Professor Nishimura.

4. Zenchū Satō entered the Myōshinji monastery in 1908, coming from Tōkeiji in Kamakura, the temple in which D. T. Suzuki used to live.

the subject into thematic presentation; though it was felt his categories were sound and helpful, it was clear he did not exhaust the possibilities, any more than does this volume. As he put it: "The Zendō life may be roughly analysed into (1) life of humility, (2) life of labour, (3) life of service, (4) life of prayer and gratitude, and (5) life of meditation. After his initiation to the Brotherhood, the monk is to be trained along these lines."[5]

Despite some overlapping in terms of materials examined, the themes which follow take quite a different tack and emerge primarily, though not exclusively, from what is observable in the drawings by Giei Satō, as interpreted by Professor Nishimura. Fundamental to each theme is a creative tension or rhythm one may find in Zen thought and practice, at their best, between various aspects of life that sometimes appear at odds. While it is easy to oversimplify this tension and to miss genuine incongruities, this is not Zen Buddhism at its best, even though it is not infrequently the guise in which this tradition is presented by Japanese and others alike. It is the premise of both commentary and introduction that these drawings capture in a unique manner the tension, rhythm, and harmony within existence to which Zen Buddhism points.

Between Monastery and Town

The monastic Zen temples of Japan, unlike their Ch'an Buddhist counterparts in China, were for the most part located in or close to urban communities. While more true of Rinzai than Sōtō forms, this phenomenon is characteristic of Zen Buddhism in general and stems to a large degree both from the time this tradition was introduced into Japan (in the early thirteenth century) and from its immediate association with aristocratic and urban-based elements within the society. Without expanding on these important historical

5. Suzuki, p.4.

factors, it is fair to ascribe a great deal of Zen's influence upon
Japanese life and culture to these beginnings, though it is an insuf-
ficient explanation of its ability to maintain and develop a creative
relationship and tension between the monastic institution and society
at large, at least among elite elements within that society.

   The drawings by Satō are mid twentieth-century impressions by one
Rinzai Zen priest of the constant rhythm one can perceive not only
between what occurs within and outside the monastery but of the
attitudes lay and ordained members of the Zen community have
toward this relationship. Most symbolic of all and typical of Buddhism
generally is the interdependence represented in the regular act of
begging (takuhatsu), which Suzuki describes as having "a two-fold
moral signification: the one is to teach the beggar humility and the
other is to make the donor accumulate the merit of self-denial."[6] Even
though less frequently practiced today than in earlier periods, for
economic and other reasons, it remains an important ingredient of
monastic life within many Zen communities.[7] Whether occurring on brief
three-hour walks through sections of the town or city or on lengthier
tours twice a year, the ultimate purpose extends beyond that of receiving
donations and is more profoundly spiritual in intent, namely, to further
each person's awareness of the interdependency of all existence, the
Buddha-nature of all sentient beings, and the inappropriateness of any
attitude but humility in the face of one's continuing attachments.
Tied to humility is the gratitude experienced when dependence is
seen as mutual, when oneness transcends separation.

   Less dramatic but no less part of the interconnection between
monastery and the wider community is the fact that most Zen priests
are located not in monastic settings but in temples and various walks of
life, many combining temple responsibilities with other vocations, that is,

6. Ibid., p.23.
7. See illustrations 24-27, 81, 85.

teaching or social work. Two of Satō's illustrations, one toward the beginning and the other at the end of the sequence, portray a priest leaving for and returning from his training as a Zen monk. The tissue connecting monastery and temple is intrinsic not simply for ordained members of the Zen community, but for the devout layman who, in his daily life, sometimes relates to the monk in his home, but, more often, to the priest in the monastery on special occasions.[8] The reciprocity of giving and receiving, on both sides, occurs in a number of formal and informal ways, ritualized and made regular in and beyond the monastery, yet occurring more profoundly in unexpected acts and words.

Works of piety alone are hardly the only connection between monastery and town. Aside from the sociability which not infrequently brings laymen and monks together, there is the inevitable business of any community, monastic or otherwise, which must be conducted. Some of the illustrations portray either a monk going into town on administrative duties or a person from the town coming to the monastery on matters of business.[9] The very alternating of responsibilities within the monastery as well, enabling some monks to meditate free of all but routine duties for a time while others work, is suggestive of this same rhythm.[10] Just as important is the fact, as Nishimura's comments indicate, that "most monks return to their home temples to aid in temple maintenance" for nearly three months during the late summer and early fall, while "a few monks remain at the monastery to help with its administrative details."[11] A more ephemeral but repeated reminder of the monastery's isolation from, yet closeness to, society is caught by Satō in his image of the swallows who nest for two months in the monastery grounds during

8. See 36, 44, 71, 79, 80, 88.
9. See 42, 45.
10. See 93.
11. See 78.

early summer, symbols both of a world beyond and of a freedom trans-
cending that of monk and layman alike. [12]

Between Change and Repetition

Central to all forms of Buddhism is the awareness of the
inseparability between constant change and repeated patterns. Deriving
from its Indian origins, yet modifying much of what it inherited, early
Buddhism emphasized with equal strength the radical newness of each
moment alongside the connection between all moments, past and
future. [13] Superimposed on this is the sensitive Japanese awareness about
the transiency of time, especially experienced in the flow of seasons
into each other, coupling expectancy with a sense of the poignant.
Found in almost all forms of traditional Japanese culture, particularly
those influenced by Zen, it is caught most graphically in the verses of
haiku, though its forms are infinite.

Without deliberately singling out this theme, the artist of these
drawings provides a host of images which portray both indigenous
Japanese and Buddhist attitudes toward time, its continuity yet
repeated freshness. The closeness to nature, reinforced by the
simplicity of monastic life, is mirrored not only in Zen gardens but
even more in a regimen geared to seasonal patterns. The yearly
calendar, divided basically in half, is filled with appropriate times
based upon the rhythms of nature and upon the needs of men in
community. [14] Both halves of the year contain as well two periods,
each three months long, enabling concentration upon the inner life to
alternate with outward expression. While a neat separation of these

---

12. See 32, 78.

13. The Japanese Buddhist term for change, mujō, is equivalent to the Sanskrit term anitya.
The Japanese word gō connotes, as does the Sanskrit karma, interrelationships between past
and future, depending on how one exercises one's freedom in the present. This concept is ex-
panded in the idea of causation, or dependent origination (Skt. pratītya-samutpāda, Jap. engi).

14. See 2, 72.

would be false to the nature of Zen, such different opportunities help to provide complementary approaches to each day, and to the year as a whole. Together they form that rhythmic harmony which is the spirit of Zen life.

No less than a third of Satō's illustrations reflect the cadences of time marked in one fashion or another in the life of Zen monks. From the delineation of dawn (and dusk) upon the palm of a monk's hand and from the successive periods of work, meditation, and refreshment, there is a ritualization of time which combines discipline with spontaneity in organic balance. Much has been written about the importance of work in monastic communities throughout the world. As Suzuki reminded us, " 'A day of no work is a day of no eating' is the literal rendering of the first rule of the monastery life."[15] Behind this counsel stand not only the physical needs of the community but the dual realization that men need to establish varied patterns of activity and that each activity has as profound a spiritual implication as the next.[16] In short, to weigh zazen more heavily than routine chores is to misunderstand zazen itself.

It is appropriate therefore that a monk-artist would devote as much attention to mundane activities as we find here. The daily rules of the monastery focus especially upon these,[17] since the fabric of social life and the self-discipline of each member are equally at stake. What strikes one especially in these sketches is the alternating rhythm between invariable patterns on the one hand and welcome relief from these on the other. "For everything there is a season" comes alive in graphic ways whether one is viewing monks rising and washing at the start of each day, or involved in preparing, cooking, and eating meals, or in the upkeep of buildings and grounds.[18]

15. Suzuki, p. 33.

16. The monastic communities of medieval Christendom had their equivalent in the saying laborare est orare.

17. See 12 and Appendix.   18. See 13, 18, 19, 23, 29, 30, 38, 44, 76, 86.

Of central importance is the stress given to bathing and cleansing of self. Related to the upkeep of the monastery as a whole and as fundamental to life as the offering and receiving of food is the purifying of body and spirit, ritualized in various forms, its import symbolized by the rite of silence observed in the act of bathing.[19] Fundamental to Japanese culture, but also consistent with traditional Buddhist views about the impurities of karma, the bath becomes peculiarly sacred within the monastic context in which the awareness of both attachment and freedom, impurity and purity, is heightened.

For both pragmatic and symbolic reasons, the days and seasons are observed in a multitude of ways: the shaving of heads every fifth day, on the days of housecleaning (shikunichi); the bimonthly days of rest (ō-shikunichi); the preparation for sesshin; the week-long sesshin themselves every sixth month; the serving of rice cakes halfway through the rainy season; the changing of robes from flax to cotton and back again twice a year; the collecting of radishes at the end of October and then pickling them for use throughout the year; the celebrations which mark the end of each three-month training period, or the coming of the winter solstice, or of the new year itself.[20] All these are occasions that both conjoin the various moments of time and provide breaks within them. Each, however trivial in itself, is "an opportunity to attain enlightenment."[21] As with the drinking of tea, it is both cere-monial and the essence of naturalness."[22] It relates to each day, yet connects all time.

Between Seriousness and Humor

The contrast between the seriousness, sometimes severity, one encounters within Zen Buddhism and the no less present humor, even hilarity,

19. See 33.
20. See 21, 31, 32, 38, 46, 72, 82, 88-91.
21. See 62.
22. See 47, 48.

is frequently misunderstood and seen as opposed. This is not to suggest that one pole or the other cannot dominate in any person or community, but only to stress that part of Zen's genius is to perceive their interrelationship. In this, both Ch'an and Zen are in continuity with much of early Buddhism, especially as portrayed in the life and teaching of Gautama, though unique Chinese and Japanese elements are incorporated by this school, making it distinct from all other forms of the Buddha Sāsana. Nowhere else in Buddhist tradition are solemnity and slapstick so juxtaposed as in the dialogs and behavior of patriarchs and masters, of those tracing their lineage through Bodhidharma (Daruma). Any communal heritage which can seriously refer to its great figures as "bundles of rags" and can advocate "killing the Buddha" not only leaves itself open to misunderstanding but intentionally forces its members to press beyond the obvious and reject all alternatives to genuine awakening.[23]

The Satō illustrations provide marvelous insight into this phenomenon. Indeed, the very artistic style employed, almost that of the cartoon, is peculiarly appropriate to the style of Zen life and practice. One thinks immediately of the omnipresent portraits of Bodhidharma whose stern-comic visage graces all Zen temples and who remains the prototype of this tension. In the West the appeal of Zen-shū has commonly been its ability to laugh at man's tendencies toward self-importance, though rarely its relentless severity. The latter is often ignored or seen as more Japanese than fundamentally Buddhist, to the great confusion of some interpreters. It would be more true to insist that authentic humor,

---

23. The following passage from the Rinzairoku is well known. "When you meet the Buddha, kill the Buddha! When you meet your ancestor, kill your ancestor! When you meet a disciple of Buddha, kill the disciple! When you meet your father and mother, kill your father and mother! When you meet your kin, kill your kin! Only thus will you attain deliverance. Only thus will you escape the trammels of material things and become free." (The Rinzairoku are the sayings of Rinzai Gigen [Lin-chi I-hsüan, d. 867], one of the greatest Ch'an masters of the T'ang dynasty. D. T. Suzuki said that they are "considered by some the supreme specimen of Zen literature.")

like joy and vitality, springs from experiences of suffering, frustrations, and death. Satō's record of the training of an unsui would be
superficial at best if it accented the fruits of enlightenment without
accenting even more the uncommonness of this experience and the
psychic pain which necessarily precedes it.

From beginning to end this diary recounts the difficulty and agony
of the journey. While the rejection that each supplicant desirous of
admission to the monastery must endure is somewhat stylized and
expected,[24] it is like nothing that he has encountered before and is but
a foretaste of the more profound rejection he will meet along the way.
The very ranking of monks according to one's time of entry reduces
prior experience or achievements to nothing in comparison with what is
now demanded. The regular shaving of heads further attests to the
realization that "experience received precedes knowledge in the
monastery."[25] If there is any central core to the diary, it lies in a series
of depictions, halfway through the collection, of monks preparing for
and enduring sesshin, with its accompanying kōans, sanzen, self-
examination, and rebukes, at the heart of which are seven strenuous
days of sitting meditation (zazen).[26]

The amount of attention devoted by Suzuki and others to the
importance of kōans, in Rinzai tradition especially, makes it unneces-
sary to elaborate here. The uniqueness of these drawings, however,
is that they provide insight into the fuller context within which
kōans, sanzen, and zazen have their place. The seriousness and the
humor of man's attempts to resolve the inexplicable, the false starts
and the frustrations generated in his efforts, and the fearsome yet
tender encouragement given by his fellow monks are captured in the
picture entitled Busshin-gyō or Great Compassion.[27] Again stylized

24. See 4-6.
25. See 31.
26. See 52-65.
27. See 58.

and cast in comic garb, the ritual of being forced to confront what each would rather avoid, namely, his own "great death," emerges as the pathway or gate toward overcoming separateness. The training week is shaped, as is the entire training of the Zen Buddhist monk, by the recognition that no freedom that refuses to experience such a death can be enduring.[28] The apparent brutality and sternness accompanying this insistence are based upon an intent which is both seasoned and compassionate, personified above all in a *Rōshi* who is implacable and gentle at the same time.

In abrupt contrast to this severity is a humaneness found throughout the monastic life. The celebration that concludes the training term; after days of hard labor the days of rest that punctuate the entire year; the recreation and the special meals; the relishing of noodles; the entertaining of adherents within the monastery itself and the being entertained by them at their homes; and, par excellence, the gay abandon of the party on winter solstice night — all reveal a dimension of Zen monastic existence that can only be experienced, and that not only relieves but complements the rigor portrayed elsewhere.[29] The most graphic scene combining both levity and the sacred is that of the monk returning from a night of saké drinking and stepping unawares upon the head of his meditating *Rōshi*. It may not be far-fetched to say that only Zen Buddhists could have imagined and treasured such a scene.[30]

Between Sounds and Silence

Typically, the monastic community has respected the eloquence

---

28. The most important training week is Rōhatsu, which commemorates Gautama's experience of bodhi, or enlightenment. Traditionally, it is believed that this occurred on December 8, so that the Rōhatsu sesshin is held during the period December 1 through 8. In a very real sense, Buddhism asserts that there is no awakening without the dispelling of attachment, ignorance, and the experience of a separate self — hence the importance of the "great death."

29. See 36, 68, 69, 71, 74, 77, 78, 82, 88–91.

30. See 96. For a perceptive treatment of the role of humor in Zen Buddhism see M. Conrad Hyers, *The Smile of the Dragon: Zen and the Comic Spirit* (London: Rider & Co., 1973).

of silence. More than most, the Zen tradition has insisted that wisdom comes only when men are reduced to silence, that without the capacity for stillness we remain deaf to most sounds. While no kōan has one meaning alone, two well known kōans symbolize Zen's inexpressibility — the sound of one hand clapping; and the plight of a man, hanging from a branch by his teeth, being asked why Bodhidharma came from the West.[31] With good reason Zen-shū cites the continuity of this "wordless Dharma" with the frequent practice of the Buddha, who, when asked questions not conducive to enlightenment, employed the method of silence. Zen's philosophic lineage can be traced in part to the Śūnyatā (kū) doctrine of early Mahāyāna, wherein all things, all doctrines are śūnya, empty or relative, a condition to be experienced most profoundly in silence but ultimately beyond it. Its indebtedness at this point to the Taoism of Lao Tzu and Chuang Tzu is also apparent, as many have noted.

As in Buddhist schools generally, the cultivation of silence in Rinzai and Sōtō, however different their emphases, is not for its own sake alone. In Rinzai, especially, there is symbolic tension between the seemingly verbal kōan and the seemingly soundless zazen, though in actuality there is equal stress upon each as a way of going beyond both. Whether in the alternating of chanting and quietness which occurs in services or in "meditation in movement" or in the rule of silence observed at meals and in bathing, there is the recognition that stillness and motion are compatible ingredients of each other. Even in the discourse (teishō) given by the Rōshi on important occasions, the real eloquence comes not through words but through the correspondence between what he says and his life, demonstrated no less by what he refrains from saying or from doing.[32]

While the distinguishability and fusion of sounds and silence are

---

31. See 22, 29.
32. See 49, 51, 61.

more apparent in monasteries set apart from urban areas, such as the head Sōtō temple of Eiheiji [33] in Fukui Prefecture, they are part of the monastic setting wherever located. Even in cities the size of Kyōto the observance of silence within certain times and places by members of the community lends to monastic life a tone and flavor which are unmistakable. The blend of sounds and quietness are as basic as the flow of seasons into each other. Liturgical sounds and meditation in quietness (shijō) produce a rhythm and balance which affect other contexts, generating deeper sensitivity both to discordancies and to harmony within the whole of life. From the ringing of a bell that rouses monks from sleep, to the sound of a gong summoning them to morning service, to the chanting and stillness with which they begin each day, there is a pattern set which helps to cultivate the ability to listen and to explore depths beyond sound. [34] The awakening to a consciousness beyond self is dependent upon developing forms of unconsciousness which paradoxically accent what one hears and afford glimpses of the Buddha-nature throughout life.

The simple and often unheard sounds of flowing water, of bird calls in the distance, or of wind through the trees are etched as vividly against the quietness as those produced by the ringing of a bell, the pounding of a drum, or the voice of the Rōshi. [35] While having as natural an appeal to cacophonous modern Japan as to the West, and while easy to sentimentalize, there are more profound implications at stake, of which these simpler or ritualized sounds are but a clue. Far from inviting an escape from the complexities of modern society, they strike a chord in man's need to discover new modes of reconciling antagonistic elements without silencing fresh attempts at expression. The hearing of new sounds and doctrines, the clear recognition of their

33. Founded by Dōgen Zenji in A.D. 1243.
34. See 13-16.
35. See 60.

relativity, and the encouragement to proceed beyond them is what quietness in the midst of confusion occasions. Satō's depiction of satori awareness toward the end of his sequence of drawings cannot be understood apart from his realistic images of man's battle with confusing sounds around him and within himself.[36] If Zen Buddhists do not succeed any better at this than do other men, they help to preserve both the necessity of the task and the possibility of the goal.

The Gateless Gate

The most characteristic tension or rhythm within Zen Buddhism may be its honoring of tradition on the one hand, and its insistence that tradition be transcended on the other. The prominence of gates leading to temples is of symbolic importance the world over, suggesting the passageway between secular and sacred. While Zen is no different from any other religion in this respect, it maintains a stark ambivalence toward not just the secular but the sacred as well. One would be blind to miss the ways in which its heritage is reverenced, but even more crucial is its caution against equating these with reality. The finger which points to the moon is not the moon. So too, the gate through which one enters into the temple or monastery is also the gate by which one returns to the world outside. The tradition itself is the Gateless Gate (Mumonkan) which prepares men to go beyond where tradition can lead them. "There is no definite gate to enter the great Way (daidō mumon)."[37]

The immense insight into human nature which this implies jibes fully with the approach of the Buddha himself, who had experienced both continuity with tradition and the need to take uncharted paths. Wandering as a lonely rhinoceros, the homeless mendicant became an early paradigm within Buddhism, though always in tandem with the communal

---

36. See 92.
37. See 3.

Sangha. The injunction by Gautama for each follower to be "a lamp unto himself" is taken as seriously by Zen Buddhists as by any of his disciples. The precarious balance between reverencing the Three Treasures (Buddha, Dharma, Sangha) and seeking enlightenment in solitude is the Gateless Gate in question.[38]

Satō's recollections of the training of an unsui are replete with illustrations of how Zen honors not only its own tradition but that of historic Buddhism. Images of the Buddha, of Bodhisattvas (especially Mañjuśrī or Monju), and of the patriarchs are reverenced with gratitude and remain as models of those who vowed to renounce everything save rescuing all sentient being.[39] Zen teaching is conveyed more through dialogs of the Masters than through any other device. The Rōshi is symbol, par excellence, of the way by which "transmission of the lamp" occurs, handed down through centuries, entrusted to those whose enlightenment frees them from dependence "on words or letters."[40] Rituals, ceremonies, and observances are no less a part of Zen heritage than of Buddhism at large.[41] The Satō drawings appropriately call attention to the respect paid to temples, monasteries, scriptures, and festivals which keep alive the tradition.[42] In many ways, particularly in the Bon Festival during August, there is a confluence also of historic Buddhism with

---

38. The symbol of the rhinoceros overlaps with part of the symbol of the unsui, though they are not identical images. The comparison with a rhinoceros occurs in the Khaggavisā-nasutta 3, 28, in Sutta-Nipāta, tr. V. Fausböll (Oxford: Clarendon Press, 1881), p. 9: "Having torn the ties, having broken the net as a fish in the water, being like a fire not returning to the burnt places, let one wander alone like a rhinoceros." In this sentence the Buddha advocates the homeless existence for those seeking nirvāna, the abandonment of all worldly claims, the freedom from attachment even in the midst of normal society.

Concerning the gateless gate, in the words of Hui-neng (A.D. 638–713): "He who does not seek the real Buddha in himself but seeks Him outside, is surely a man of great delusion." See Wing-tsit Chan, tr., The Platform Sutra (New York: St. John's University Press, 1963), p. 147.

39. See 8, 15-17.

40. See 10, 83. The latter commentary contains the full quatrain of Bodhidharma's, from which these quoted phrases are taken.

41. See 35.

42. See 34, 40, 70, 83, 84, 87, 89-91, 95.

indigenous practice and belief in Japan,[43] providing a richness and texture to the religious life without which Zen might seem abstract to the common man.

This honoring of gates, leading men beyond where they are, is combined with a ruthless rejection of all gates as final. Both are at the core of the monastic experience, preparing persons primarily not for a life of separation from the rest of existence but for total yet emancipated involvement with it. The symbols of separation (begging bowl, monk's robes, head-shaving razor) point toward a separation not from other men but from one's own attachments and ignorance. The essence of each teishō given by the Rōshi is to cultivate the strenuous methods of the patriarchs not for their own sake but to experience the same freedom which these figures embodied.[44] The great death, without which no awakening occurs, is of everything but awareness of one's nonseparate ego. It enables one to be, in fact, an unsui, or Zen trainee, who wanders from the monastery to seek the way, like clouds and water, in search of truth.[45]

Bardwell L. Smith

43. See 79-80.
44. See 49.
45. See also Kōji Sato, The Zen Life, photographs by Sosei Kuzunishi, translated by Ryojun Victoria (New York, Tokyo, Kyōto: Weatherhill/Tankosha, 1972).

Unsui

A Diary of Zen Monastic Life

1. Unsui nikki   Daily Life of an Unsui

The word *unsui* refers to a monk undergoing Zen training; the Chinese characters can be translated literally as "cloud, water," pointing to two aspects of the Zen monk's life. The first, which is the origin of this term, is that monks in training gather around a great Zen Master as water or clouds gather in certain places. The second is that the monks live their lives so smoothly that they can be compared to a moving cloud or to running water.

This picture in which, on the left, we meet the central character in the following narration, suggests the importance of daily tasks in the monastic life. "Meditation in movement has a thousand times more value than meditation in stillness." This well-known phrase captures the Zen spirit. The title of this collection also demonstrates the emphasis on regularity and on the ordinary, both of which characterize Zen Buddhism.

2. Angya   Leaving the Home Temple

The young unsui, who grew up in a local temple as a disciple
(deshi) of the old temple priest, is here leaving his master-father
(shishō) for his formal training in a Zen monastery (zendō or sōdō).
Twice a year new monks are allowed to enter the monastery at the
beginning of the training term. The Zen monastic year is divided into
two periods: a summer or rainy term from May to October, and a winter
or snow term from November to April. Both terms consist of a three-
month retreat and a three-month pilgrimage.

When traveling, each monk wears a formal robe. In the front bundle
he keeps his seasonal robes and kimonos; on top of the bundle are fastened
Buddhist scriptures, bowls for his meals (jihatsu), and a head-shaving
razor. The small bundle on his back is an old-fashioned raincoat. The hat
in his hand is worn by the Zen monk whenever he leaves the monastery; it
is designed to block his view of the outer world and to concentrate his
consciousness within his own being as he walks through the city.

3. Kashaku   Arriving at a Monastery

Each monk is entirely free in the selection of a monastery. Choosing the right Zen Master is essential for the novice monk, as it will affect everything that follows. In Japan today, about forty monasteries belong to Rinzai Zen Buddhism. In each monastery as many as twenty or thirty monks, or as few as two or three, live together. Zen communities for nuns are separate, but their daily rules are similar to those for monks.

On the tablet hung on the gate is the monastery's name and the Zen text that is commented upon by the Zen Master every five days throughout the term. Although it is said, "There is no definite gate to enter the great Way (daidō mumon), or as the title on the tablet says, Gateless Gate (Mumonkan), this physical gate of the monastery stands imposingly before the new monk.

4. Niwa-zume   Asking Permission to Enter

Zen Buddhism believes that a journey to the truth must begin with one's own decision and that it is achieved through one's own efforts. Therefore, a new monk should be pushed back instead of invited. As with an ox that comes to the riverside voluntarily to drink, after having been kept away from the river, it is better that he drink the water of his own accord than for him to be pulled forcibly.

The elder monk is refusing to receive the unsui into the monastery. Sometimes the new monk is thrown out of the gate, which is then closed behind him. No matter how difficult this test may be, the new monk must endure it. He must keep a bowing posture for two days at the front step of the entrance hall. In the lower left corner of the drawing is written "Look beneath your feet." To take off one's shoes in an orderly manner is the outer meaning; the more important inner teaching is to look underneath our outer, external existence.

5. Tanga　Staying Overnight as a Guest

After remaining an entire day in bowing posture, the new monk is allowed to stay in the monastery overnight in a small guest room (tanga-ryō). For the new monk, this first night in the monastery is a most impressive one. He is allowed no lamp after dark. Soon an old monk comes in quietly with a candle stand, serves him a cup of tea, and asks him to sign the guest book.

Until nine o'clock that night, the monk has to meditate facing the wall before he can go to bed. He is given only a wide mattress which he folds in two, lying on the bottom half and pulling the top half over him.

The next day after breakfast he must once more go outside the monastery gate and remain in bowing posture the whole day at the entrance.

6. Tanga-zume　　Examination in the Guest Room

　　　　After a two-day probation period, the new monk is led to the small guest room, where he must meditate in a cross-legged position for five days. This is obviously a much harder discipline than the niwa-zume examination. Because this small room is in an isolated place, there is never any activity around it.

　　For a young monk who has enjoyed his youth in amusement and in discussion with his friends, to be alone in silence is a difficult experience. His mind fills with fond images of his past life. The walls and sliding doors around him appear to have a thousand eyes from the elder monks. If he is lazy he is rejected by the monastery and must begin all over again.

7. Shika   Greeting the Head Monk

During each of these five days, the novice must go after breakfast to the quarters where the head monk (shika) lives, to greet him and to thank him for his hospitality. In this way the head monk comes to know the new monk, but the latter is not yet allowed to become a brother of the monastery.

The official task of the shika is to regulate the monastic life in general and to entertain guests who visit the monastery. Usually he has had at least ten years of experience in Zen meditation in the same monastery and has advanced beyond the other monks in both meditation and his daily life.

8. Sandō   Entering the Meditation Hall

After seven days of successful examination, the monk is allowed
to become a brother in the monastery. He is led to the meditation hall
(zendō), usually located in the innermost part of the monastery. This
hall, sometimes called the "Buddha-selecting place" (sembutsu-jō), is
on the average thirty feet wide by sixty feet long. Set along the wall is
a platform (tan) two or three feet high, which can accommodate about
thirty monks. On the tablet hung above the head of each monk is
written his name. The front entrance is used only for formal occasions,
the back entrance for informal daily use.

Near the front entrance the Bodhisattva Mañjuśrī (Monju Bosatsu),
a Buddhist guardian of Wisdom, is enshrined. The novice comes into the
hall, greets the image of Monju and promises not to leave this place until
he has achieved his purpose of Zen training.

9. Antan   Assignment of Living Space

A tatami mat, three and a half feet wide and seven feet long, a sufficient area on which to meditate and sleep, is provided for the monk's living purposes. The wood railing in front is used as a table for meals during the weeks of special training and as a pillow at night. Each monk keeps his daily equipment in a box set against the wall. Above, there is a shelf on which he keeps his bowls, razor, and scripture; over the shelf, the sleeping mattress, hidden by a curtain, is kept.

In the monastic life the monk's ranking is strictly according to the time he entered the monastery; age and academic degree are of no significance. Experience is regarded as the primary measure of a monk's rank, and he is continually surprised by what is taught.

10. Shōken   Meeting with the Zen Master

Finally, the novice is given the honor of meeting his Zen Master (Rōshi). To the new monk who has thus far endured the hard examination, the Master seems very kind. With a great smile, the Master asks the monk about his purpose in coming to the monastery and promises to do all he can to help lead the monk to the hoped-for awareness. The monk presents a small amount of money "for incense" in order to establish the relationship of Master and disciple.

Among more than ten thousand Rinzai priests, about one hundred are known as Zen Masters and are called Rōshi. Each is believed to be a fully awakened man and to have been certified as such by his Master. In this way "transmission of the lamp" is regarded as most important within Zen tradition. There is a definite genealogical tree on which each monk can trace his genealogy from the time of Gautama Buddha.

11. Kaihan   Announcing the Time of Day

At the front entrance of the meditation hall an oaken board (han) is hung. On the board is written: "Matter of life and death is great. Time runs quickly; nothing remains; it waits for no man. You should not waste your time."

The board is struck three times daily to announce the time. The first announcement is at dawn, when a monk goes outside and looks at his hand. According to the rule, it is dawn when the lines in his palm become visible. He strikes the board, and the sound echoes beautifully from the surrounding mountains, stirring the monks for the beginning of a new day.

To begin the night session, the second announcement occurs at dusk, when the lines of the palm disappear. At nine o'clock in the evening the third time is announced; this marks the day's ending.

12. Kiku   Rules for the Daily Routine

Above the back entrance of the meditation hall is hung
a large tablet on which the severe daily rules of the monastic
life are written. They deal not only with zazen meditation but
also with seemingly trivial actions such as how to walk, how to
drink tea, how to take off sandals. The daily rules are purposely very
strict to put the monk's life in good order so that his inner being may
attain right awareness. For this reason, the initiate's daily life is
filled with admonitions from elder monks.

The last of the written rules is that anyone not following them
is obstructing the progress of others and must be removed from
the monastery without recourse.

13. Kaijō   Rising in the Morning

At three-thirty each morning in summer (four-thirty in winter) the monks are awakened by the ringing of a small bell. They rise quickly and go out the back entrance of the hall to wash. Every morning water is poured into a basin for the entire day's use by all thirty monks. Each monk may use no more than three bamboo cups of water for himself. He holds the cup in one hand and washes his face with the other, like a cat. For the initiate who may have used unlimited water at his home temple this is disconcerting. The specific teaching of not wasting comes from the Zen Master Dōgen (1200-1253), who once advised, "Use two cups and save one for your descendants."

The beginning of the day is a very busy time; our friend is hurrying to use the toilet.

14. Shuttō   Going to the Main Hall for Morning Services

Within a monastery announcements are made by various means. When the monks return to the meditation hall from washing themselves, the front entrance is opened. From the sound of opening doors, monks already inside the main hall (hondō) know it is time to strike the gong. On hearing this, the other monks, now wearing their surplices, proceed to the main hall for morning service.

Outside, it is still dark; the monks walk quietly in the fresh morning air. The elder monks stand at each corner, watching the new monk's steps. It is said that the way a monk walks reveals his state of mind. An initiate walks carelessly; sometimes too fast, at other times too slovenly. Elder monks walk quickly, yet quietly.

15. Chōka   Morning Services

In the main hall the images of the Buddha and of the patriarchs are enshrined; they are reverenced because they represent awakened man, not because they are idols. Each brother kneels very deeply, as shown by the Zen Master in the center, to show his thanks for the dharma which has been found and handed down through the patriarchs; and second, to demonstrate his own vow to achieve the same awareness his ancestors did for him, and to transmit it to his descendants.

While the monks chant scripture for thirty minutes, an elder monk walks around and encourages them, for, in this early morning hour, encouragement is not uncalled for.

16. Dōnai fugin   Chanting Scripture in the Meditation Hall

Returning to the meditation hall, the monks chant scripture for their guardian, Monju Bosatsu. While they have been at morning service, this hall has been cleaned by two monks. It is refreshing to chant scripture in a clean hall made fragrant by incense, which is burned in a small stand beside the eldest monk (jikijitsu) during the period of zazen. A stick of incense takes forty-five minutes to burn; in this way the duration of the meditation period is determined. An interval of fifteen minutes exists between the two periods.

After the chanting of scripture, a tea made with plum seed and a little sugar is served as the ceremony for the beginning of each day. This drink, called baitō, keeps the monks in good physical condition.

17. Jōjū fugin Chanting Scripture in the Administrative Quarters

At the beginning of each term about ten monks are selected by the master for various official duties, such as attendants (sannō or inji) to the Master, providing hospitality for visitors, attendants (fuzui) to the head monk, cooking (tenzo), and taking care of the monks in the meditation hall.

These official monks live in quarters separate from the meditation hall. They are severely regulated by the monastic rules for daily life, and meditate in movement rather than in quietness in the meditation hall. After returning from morning service in the main hall, they chant scripture for the guardian deity enshrined in the administrative quarters. So many guardians in a Zen monastery may seem unusual, but this is an example of how Zen Buddhism historically has been mixed with various aspects of Japanese popular religion.

18. Tenzo — Cooking Quarters

    Food is a most important part of daily life. In the monastery the elder monks are the cooks; they wake up earlier than the other monks to make breakfast. To prepare soft-cooked rice (kayu) for thirty persons, as the monk in the center of the picture is doing, takes time and good technique.

    In the monastery today, monks still use chopped wood for cooking, though they may not be too free in using it — burning dried leaves instead as much as possible. Food must also be conserved — a grain of rice is thought to have the same value as Mount Sumeru, the holiest of mountains in the Indian Buddhist world-view. Or, again, it is taught that the monk should regard his daily food as being as valuable as his eyes.

    The monk at the right is striking a gong to announce that breakfast is now ready.

19. Handaikan   Waiting on Table in the Dining Room

Every monk takes his turn as a waiter. As the dining room is usually located near the entrance to the monastery, the monks in the meditation hall must walk a long distance to reach it. While just the smell of the food is attractive to hungry monks, the meal itself is very frugal. At breakfast, for example, a monk is allowed only three bowls of rice, pickled plums, and vegetables. The rice is brought to the dining room in the right-hand bucket, pickles in the shallow bucket, and the vegetables in the third, tall bucket. The container on the left is used for collecting leftover rice, called saba, which is first offered to the spirits and will then be put on the kitchen veranda for birds, who will soon come to eat it.

20. Shukuza　Breakfast

　　Breakfast begins with the chanting of scripture. As they chant, the monks uncover their bowls and arrange them in a straight line under the direction of the head monk. The dining room is one of three places for silence, the other two being the meditation hall and the bath. No one is allowed to speak or make any sound, even when biting into a radish pickle.

　　The waiter watches the shika very carefully, to know when to commence the next course. At the end of the meal the monks again chant scripture. Even for the poorest meal, the monk must show deep thanks. A Japanese philosopher has written that meals in Zen monasteries are even worse than those in prisons.

21. Sarei   Tea Ceremony and Daily Announcements

After returning from breakfast, the monks are served a cup of tea. This ceremony is one of the most important events in monastic life because drinking tea together cultivates the harmony of group life. It also serves as an attendance check on the monks, whose presence is required.

Besides this morning tea ceremony, once in a while there is another ceremony (sōzarei) in which all members of the monastery come together with the Master. Twice a month, as well, there is a tea ceremony at which all the administrative monks meet for consultation.

Following the tea ceremony each morning, the daily schedule is announced. Tasks consist of begging in the town, working in the garden, attending the Master's lecture, and cleaning up monastery buildings and grounds.

22. Dokusan   Daily Consultation with the Master

Every morning after the tea ceremony, the monk comes to the Master for sanzen consultation. The Master, according to each monk's degree and state of mind, gives the monk a kōan, an irrational problem solved only through deep experience. Our friend seems to have been given the first kōan, well-known as "Master Hakuin's sound of one hand clapping." Hakuin once said to a monk, "Listen to the sound of one hand clapping." We can make a sound by clapping both hands together, but how is it possible with only one? A kōan is not like a mathematical problem, to be solved by means of our intellect. Instead, it is a means used to help a man break through his small ego, to become aware of his real self. Eighteen hundred kōans are systematized in Rinzai Zen today. To become a Master, a monk is expected to solve them all. This takes ten to fifteen years, at the very least.

23. Nitten sōji   Daily Cleaning of the Garden

"A day without work is a day without food." In line with this strict monastery rule, the daily cleaning of the garden after sanzen has an important role in monastic life. Each monk concentrates his consciousness on the given kōan while working.

To clean the environment is also to cleanse the mind. The monk sweeping the garden can remind us of the famous story of the Ch'an or Zen Master Hsiang-yen (Kyōgen) who, when in the so-called state of darkness, was absorbed in a kōan while sweeping a garden. A small stone was tossed up by his broom and hit a bamboo. At that very moment, Hsiang-yen achieved awareness of his real self. Such a small event in daily life can become an important moment of awareness for one who is in great darkness.

24. Shūmai   Visiting Adherents to Receive Donations

Once a month monks visit the houses of adherents to receive rice or money for the support of monastic life. This adherent seems pleased to donate, but the costume of the monk is so old-fashioned that the dog barks.

Once Master Chao-chou (Jōshū, 778-897) was asked, "Does a dog have Buddha-nature?" and he answered, "Mu" (nothing). Since Buddha taught that all beings, without exception, possess the Buddha-nature, why then does this dog not have it? (This is a kōan given to new monks.) To this monk, however, the dog seems to be without the Buddha-nature, as long as he barks at him.

From early morning to late evening the monk must walk great distances, and through this experience he comes to realize how precious is each donation.

25. Takuhatsu   Begging in the Streets

The first, third, sixth, and eighth of every month (plus all other dates containing those digits) are the days for begging. All the monks leave the monastery in groups of three and go to different parts of town for three hours in the morning. They do not stand in front of each door, but walk along the road saying in a friendly manner, "*Hō . . . u*," which means "the rain of Dharma."

Hearing this from a distance people emerge from their homes and donate small amounts of money or rice. The monks receive it, bowing deeply. To bow, especially to a small child, is good discipline for breaking down one's ego. Moreover, to receive this sincere donation from common people encourages the monk to train himself for the benefit of all sentient beings. All donations are collected into one box and used for the monks' daily maintenance.

小
憩

26. Shōkei   Brief Rest while Begging

Begging in a loud voice is so strenuous that monks become very tired and hungry. They are often invited to stop to rest by an adherent or a temple priest who knows the monks' life well. They are served tea, which they receive without hesitation — a good example of how giving and receiving are in natural harmony. In Buddhist teaching, the practice of giving is among the great disciplines. It requires devotion of the entire self to those around one. The monk's begging practice, therefore, is an important opportunity for common people also to practice this devotion.

Once Master Hakuin was begging in town. He was so deeply absorbed in a kōan that he was not conscious of where he was going. Upon walking into an ox in the street, he was immediately awakened to his real self. In this way, even begging in town is seen as a central part of monastic life.

帰
院

27. Kiin Returning to the Monastery

  The monks return from begging and chant scripture for the guardian of the living quarters, demonstrating their thanks for completing the sacred task, and promising not to waste the donations of sincere people. Begging can be a sacred practice by which a monk can break his ego and by which the people as well are given a chance to break their egos. The practice of begging, in this sense, is an ideal practice of Mahāyāna Buddhism, by which one seeks upwardly for the awareness of self and downwardly for the salvation of all sentient beings. On the lid of the monastery's money box is written, "A wise man loves money, yet he knows the right way (Tao) to use it."

28. Saiza   Lunch

At lunch no one receives a bowl of pure rice — rather, three parts of rice mixed with seven parts of wheat, plus miso soup, vegetables, and pickles. This is the biggest meal of the day. Supper is not viewed as a meal, but as "medicine," and is composed of leftovers from lunch. Before lunch the monks chant scripture and a five-part vow:

1. Let us think on how much we have accomplished and how this food has come to us.
2. Let us accept this prepared food only because we have now performed good deeds.
3. Let us take only enough food to satisfy our needs, leaving our hunger not quite satisfied.
4. Let us partake of this food as medicine in order to aid our thin bodies.
5. Let us accept this food so that we may establish our way.

The waiter is collecting leftovers which are first offered to the spirits and then given to birds or fish.

29. Samu   Working in the Garden

Almost every day, except during the week set aside for intensive training, the monks are assigned some work-project in the afternoon. Gathering fuel for cooking meals or heating bath water is one of the most necessary daily tasks. As we know, work is another opportunity for monks to meditate and become awakened to their real selves. The two monks on the left are imitating the following kōan which appears in the Mumonkan (Gateless Gate):

Zen Master Hsiang-yen once said, "Suppose a man climbed a tree and held onto a branch not with his hands and feet but with his mouth biting a branch. If a person should come along and ask him the meaning of Bodhidharma's coming from the West (the essence of Zen), how should he answer? If he does not answer, he will betray the man's trust, but if he does answer, he will lose his own life."

30. Enju   Growing Vegetables

  In the monastery the monks eat vegetables only from their own garden. Through this work-project they can experience the "grace of heaven" and also give thanks for what is donated to them in their begging, since it comes without hard work on their part. This is the place where each monk concentrates on one simple task assigned him.

  Meditation in movement thus demonstrates how Zen training is different from forms of quietism or from the purely speculative life. It provides a good change of pace for the monks who are mainly involved in sitting meditation in the zendō.

31. Teihatsu   Shaving the Head

Approximately every fifth day — each date containing the digits four or nine (shikunichi) — is used as a day of housecleaning. This day begins with shaving one another's heads. The shaved head was originally a symbol of a monk's strong will to break from secular illusions and delusions. It is not simple for the novice to get used to shaving his head; older monks do it skillfully and quickly. Even in such a minor task, a new monk can realize how experience precedes knowledge in the monastery. After shaving, the monks clean the monastery grounds, bathe, and wash their clothes. To cleanse their environment in this fashion causes each monk to experience an entirely fresh feeling, invigorating him to continue his Zen training.

32. Ō-shikunichi   Day of Rest

　　　The fourteenth and the last days of each month are
days of rest. The monks may stay in bed late into the morning
if they desire, but they also shave their heads and clean up generally inside and outside the hall. This is a scene of cleaning the toilet;
there is a guardian, enshrined above the entrance, to safeguard this
room from harm. To clean such a place, which ordinary people find
distasteful to do, is good training for the monk toward his goal of
selflessness.

　　In the afternoon the monks are allowed to go about their private
needs and tasks. In the early summer swallows come to Japan,
nesting for two months in the monastery grounds, becoming good
friends of the monks, and bringing to their cloistered life something
of the free world outside.

33. Kaiyoku   Taking a Bath

On every cleaning day two monks have the task of preparing the bath. They must heat the water with only a limited supply of fuel—a difficult job for the novice. Here the teaching to waste nothing is actually experienced. Before and after bathing, the monks bow to the guardian who himself attained satori as he was about to bathe. Since the bath is one of the three silent rooms in the monastery, the monks are not allowed even to whisper or to laugh. They must concentrate on removing their secular dust, which so easily accumulates from daily existence.

34. *Shukushin* Going to Services at the Head Temple

On the first and fifteenth of every month, Zen temples throughout Japan have services to celebrate the well-being of the nation. The monks go to the Buddha hall (*Butsuden*) of the head temple of their school to participate. The setting of this temple is like a Chinese painting of the Southern School. Joining in this ceremony twice every month is a helpful and refreshing experience for each monk.

35. Gyōdō   Ceremony in the Main Hall

People are sometimes surprised to see Zen monks engaged
in such an elaborate ceremony. The main hall is decorated in a
manner similar to that of a Catholic church, with images, candles, and
other decorations. Priests of the various temples wear colorful robes
and chant long scriptures. While chanting, they walk around the
hall, following the Rōshi. This provides those adherents who attend
this ceremony with a strong impression of the Zen tradition.

The Buddha image is worshipped, however, in a rather special
way, principally by the expression of thanks for having received this
wonderful means to realize truth and by the promise to attain this
truth themselves, in order to transmit it to their descendants.

36. Tenjin   Visiting a Layman's Home

Monks are sometimes invited to the homes of families supporting the monastery, usually on their return from begging. They gladly accept a delicious meal, since this is their only chance to really satisfy their hunger. Here our friend is polishing off a bowl of rice; his fellow monk is impressed by his capacity. This is an enjoyable experience for the novice, though the hostess often worries because the monks eat rapidly and the food disappears quickly. Lay people like to serve monks, however, since they and their ancestors may gain merit from this good deed.

晚
課

37. Banka   Evening Services

At four in the afternoon the monastery gate is closed and the monks chant scripture in the main hall. The new monk often finds the rapid chanting difficult to follow, but elder monks are accustomed to the speed and are able to concentrate on the meaning. They have already acquired the spirit which the scripture expresses in the chanting. For the mature monk, in contrast to the initiate, the chanting is only a secondary task and is not difficult at all to perform.

38. Banka sōji　Evening Cleaning

Monks must clean not only the meditation hall but also the many other monastery buildings. These buildings therefore shine brilliantly because of constant cleaning throughout many generations. Even monastery life is being modernized, as illustrated here by a monk's using a mop, formerly regarded as an extravagant piece of equipment.

The discipline of cleaning and maintaining the monastery grounds in good order is considered very important for controlling and improving the state of one's mind.

39. Konshō   Evening Bell

When twilight begins, the evening bell is struck by a monk who simultaneously chants scripture. The knobs on the bell number one hundred and eight, which, according to Buddhist teaching, is the number of man's delusions. Buddhists believe that by striking such a bell one can discard a delusion with each stroke. On New Year's Eve about fifty thousand Buddhist temples throughout Japan strike their temple bells a hundred and eight times to cast out the delusions man has acquired during the past year.

40. Shuya　Fire Watch

At nine in the evening as the monks chant scripture before
retiring, one monk tours the monastery courtyard to detect any fires.
In accordance with Japanese custom, he strikes wood blocks
together as he walks around the buildings. Keeping a careful
watch for fires is a first in the many written daily rules; everywhere in the
living quarters may be found cautions about fire. Many of the
temple buildings are important cultural properties that are
associated with great personalities and precious historical
traditions. One is reminded of the ancient saying that the outbreak
of fire is even worse than the breaking of a precept.

41. Kaichin Going to Bed

After a long day, the monk is left entirely free at last.
In an early Zen text it is recorded that formerly Zen monks never
lay down throughout their entire lives. They slept in a sitting
posture, resting their chins on a long board. Following this tradition,
monks in the monastery are provided no pillow. They are given only
one mat, which they fold in two so that they can sleep between the
halves. However austere their lives, they exercise their freedom to
some extent in the dark meditation hall by the individual arrange-
ments of their mats and "pillows." Even in the midst of winter, however,
they are given neither heater nor socks.

42. Fūsu Bookkeeper

At the end of each month merchants come to collect their bills. The bookkeeper of the monastery must be very careful with the crafty merchant; here, he is complaining about bad merchandise. Zen Master Hakuin used to say, "You would do better to engage in trade by using both hands than to listen to the sound of one hand clapping." A good merchant becomes a listener to one hand clapping.

三応

43. Sannō   Attending the Master

The monks who attend the Rōshi are very busy, for they must serve his meals, prepare him for consultation, entertain visiting guests, and follow him when he goes out. An attendant must devote all his energies to the Master, as a son to his father.

The Rōshi is often asked by his followers to write samples of his calligraphy. To make the ink (sumi) for calligraphy is difficult, but merely to watch the Master's manner of writing is a compensating privilege, for his movements seem different from those of ordinary calligraphers. He uses no special technique, but expresses his Zen spirit in vital, spontaneous movements.

44. Shussai   Serving Zen Dishes to Adherents

Monastery food consists primarily of vegetables, often combined into unique dishes, created through the monks' own innovations. Adherents are sometimes invited to the monastery and served many dishes which they have never seen before. These are actually made from what ordinary people throw away (for example, the leaves of radishes, scraps of greens, or mashed bean curd) and are fried in oil to give them an excellent taste. The monk making a wry face is mashing sesame seeds to make a paste, the favorite of all vegetable dishes in a Zen monastery. It is strange that almost all monks gain weight on a vegetable diet. Since lacquered bowls are used only for formal occasions in the monastery, apparently a special event is depicted here.

45. *Fuzui*　　*Attending the Head Monk*

　　The shika usually has two monks serving as his secretaries, who frequently go out on business. The secretary monk is going out in the rain to shop and three monks are just returning from their tour of begging. Even on stormy days the daily schedule of the monastery is not altered. A secretary also does not hesitate to help monks who are in training.

46. Hashin kyūji   Mending and Moxa

During the two retreat periods of the monastic year (May 1–
July 31 and November 1 – January 31) there are several weeks set
aside for intensive training. But before the training begins, the
monks have a day of rest and preparation. They mend and wash their
clothes, and make sure that they will be in good health for the
coming week. In former days the monks burned moxa (mogusa)
on their legs and back, but today they share the benefits of
modern life and use plasters instead. Such a peaceful day
passes rapidly.

茶礼出頭

47. Sarei shuttō　Gathering for a Tea Ceremony

On the eve of the new term a tea ceremony is performed by the Rōshi for all monks in the monastery, an occasion on which no one may be absent. At the sound of large wooden clappers, all residents gather in the main hall wearing the white socks reserved for special occasions. When all have taken their seats, the Rōshi enters quietly, followed by the head monk carrying a candlestand. The Rōshi then sits on a red carpet in the highest place in the main hall. This scene is so solemn that it creates an atmosphere of formality.

48. Sōzarei　Tea Ceremony for the Entire Monastery

This tea ceremony is not simply a ritual but the most important event in the monastic life, as it indicates the passing of time and causes the monk to rededicate himself to the careful use of the period just ahead. The monks are allowed to drink the same tea as the Master, making them feel close to him and to each other. The ceremony thus has a deep significance for establishing good relationships and harmony.

亀
鑑

49. Kikan   Master's Address of Encouragement

After the conclusion of the tea ceremony, the Master gives an encouraging address, the content of which has remained essentially the same throughout the history of this particular monastery. The following is a sample of such an address:

For the student of Zen Buddhist practice, it is very important to cultivate the strenuous methods of the patriarchs. Nevertheless, many ignorant fellows in our time ignore such an important thing, forget the patriarchs' toil, waste worthwhile time, and are proud only of staying in the monastery. What a sorrowful thing! You who train yourself in my monastery, study hard on each kōan. Concentrate carefully until the resulting mass of doubt is broken, so that you may jump from the cave of life and death and experience the spirit which the patriarchs experienced before you. If you can accomplish this, you will enjoy your own self-emancipation and will thank the Buddha for his gift of excellent teaching. How can we spend our life without this experience of rapture? Study hard. Study hard.

50. Kokuhō   Informal Encouragement

Sometimes, in the middle of the night, the novice is called outside the meditation hall and reproached by elder monks for his carelessness during the day. This is a terrible hour for the new monk, but for an honest monk it is a very helpful encouragement from his elders, who have had far richer experience than himself. For a dishonest monk, it is a severe lesson in selflessness. Though this method in group training is harsh, it is effective in helping the monks polish each other, as a diamond is polished by rubbing against other diamonds.

51. Kaikō Opening Discourse by the Master

On May first, the rainy-season, or strict, term begins, lasting until the end of July. Just before the end of April, the monastery was on vacation and the monks were allowed to relax. All former monks of the monastery are invited to the first in a series of discourses (teishō) given by the Master at the initial ceremony. From then on, the monks may not go out privately. They chant scripture for the Buddha, the patriarchs, and for the author of the text on which the Master discourses, expressing thanks for the teaching and vowing to attain their own goals. To the initiate, the Master appears as awesome as a lion roaring in the forest.

52. Sesshin   Week of Special Training

At the entrance is hung a tablet announcing that the monastery is in a special training week, and that visitors cannot now see the Master or the monks. During each month of the two retreat terms there is a special training week, flanked by one week of pretraining and one of post training. During the special training weeks monks are engaged only in meditation; during the two accompanying weeks they are given work-projects in the garden.

坐禪

53. Zazen   Sitting Meditation

An original text on zazen teaches one to sit as follows:

When one wishes to begin zazen, he places a thick cushion in a quiet place, wears his robe and belt loosely, and puts all things about him in good order. Then he sits with his legs crossed in the lotus position. First, one places the right foot over the left thigh, then the left foot over the right thigh; or, one may sit in a half-crossed sitting position, in which only the left foot rests upon the right thigh. Secondly, one places the right hand on the left foot, palm facing upward; then the left hand on the right palm so that the faces of the thumbs push against each other. Then, gradually, one raises the body, moving it backwards and forwards, to the left and to the right, to secure a balanced sitting posture for the body. . . . Keep ears and shoulders, nose and navel parallel to one another. The tongue should touch the upper jaw while both the lips and teeth are kept closed; the eyes should remain slightly open so that one avoids falling asleep. . . . Once the physical posture has been well-ordered, one should regulate the breath by pushing forward the abdomen.

54. Shijō　Meditation in Complete Quietness

The head monk (jikijitsu) of the meditation hall regulates the meditation by sounding a small bell or a wooden clapper. He measures time by an incense stick which burns for forty-five minutes. While the monks are in shijō, they may not leave the meditation hall and must maintain a state of high tension. The associate head monk walks around the hall very quietly, and when he finds a monk dozing reproves him with the "encouraging stick" (keisaku). Even in the summer monks are not permitted to brush away a mosquito or dry their perspiration. They are taught that when a man is concentrating on a kōan, he should have no consciousness of physical discomfort. As shown here, some lay people also join in the sesshin, which literally means "gathering one's thoughts."

55. Keisaku   Encouragement

This action may appear to be a very violent and harsh method of encouragement, but such is not the case. When a monk is meditating and finds himself becoming sleepy, he asks the encouraging monk to strike him severely on his back. Three blows are given on each side in the rainy season, and five blows in winter. Before the striking, each monk bows to the other, making sure the action is taken only as encouragement and not through personal resentment. The blows must be given without hesitation or reservation; in fact, their administration is a great discipline in freeing the monks from private feelings. One finds here a certain kind of group mysticism, a sense of helping one another attain awareness.

喚
鐘

56. Kanshō   Summons from the Master

Several times a day the Master calls the monks individually for consultation, at which time each must reply to the kōan given him. To find a possible answer to an irrational kōan is no simple task. The monks wait at the entrance to the Master's room with uncertain and fearful feelings. Some have very vivid expressions that result from their awakened minds and are eager for the Master's agreement and congratulations. But, for most monks, waiting is only twenty minutes of oppressive silence.

入
室

57. Nisshitsu   Entering the Master's Room

The room used for consultation with the Master is sometimes
called the "Battlefield of the Dharma Truth." After the monk concludes
his deep bow in front of the Master, he is on an equal level to discuss
the dharma truth. This is particularly significant, for the monk may
use whatever behavior is necessary to express his experience of this
truth. He may even strike the Master's cheek or ride upon his back, but
the Master does not hesitate to strike the monk with the Zen stick or
to throw him from the room. In fact, the Master sometimes refuses a
monk entry into his room, since from the monk's gait he can judge the
state of his mind. The dialog between the two is concluded by the
sound of a bell, signaling the next monk to enter. Notice our friend's
earnest expression; he is about to reply to the kōan concerning one
hand clapping. The Master, however, appears unimpressed.

58. Busshin-gyō　Great Compassion

Sometimes a monk refuses to enter the Master's room because he can think of no more possible answers to his kōan. The elder monks then force him to face the Master, and the meditation hall suddenly becomes a violent place. Even though the monk has no answer, he must enter the Master's room, receive his rebuke, and then go back to the meditation hall. In this way the monk can reach that crucial state of mind necessary for satori. Through such encouragement or compassion a monk comes to the state of "great death," in which there is no consciousness, a state of absolute oneness where no consciousness of himself or his physical environment is experienced. The face of the monk entering such a state loses its expression and becomes masklike. Without such a "death" he cannot break through to true awareness.

59. Kinhin   Meditation while Walking

About every three hours the monks walk around the meditation hall for relaxation, retaining their spirit of Zen while doing so. This is the very important practice of meditation in movement. The palm of one hand is placed over the back of the other; both are then pressed tightly against the chest as the monk moves. Zen texts insist that the monk walk very slowly, perhaps three steps for each breath. Today, however, in most Rinzai monasteries the monks sometimes run rapidly, to emphasize that Zen is not quietism.

法
鼓

60. Hokku   Dharma Drum

The dharma drum is beaten to announce the occasion of the Master's discourse on a Zen text. The monks then enter the hall and take their places, followed finally by the Master. The sound of the drum is like thunder and calls the dragon (usually painted on the ceiling of the dharma hall in a Zen temple), who is regarded in Indian tradition as the guardian of Bodhidharma, the bringer of rain, and the symbol of celebration. Standing in the center of the monks, the Master seems like a lion or perhaps king of the forest.

61. Teishō — Discourse on a Zen Text

The Master's discourse is not so much a lecture as a demonstration; he does not interpret the sentences of the text, but comments from his own experience as an awakened person. Most of the monks fail to understand his demonstration and often succumb to sleep. The more mature monks, however, who have had an experience of awareness, are able to identify with the Master's teishō. No one may write down what is said, but each is expected to receive the demonstration into his whole body and mind.

工
夫

62. Kufū Resourcefulness

    Each moment of the monastic life is seen as an
opportunity to attain enlightenment. Even the small, trivial tasks
are not looked down upon, for the resolution of a kōan can
sometimes be obtained by making a straw sandal or a bamboo
broom, by taking care of the garden, or by chopping wood for fuel.

63. Yaza   Individual Meditation at Night

After the lights of the monastery are turned off, each monk privately leaves the meditation hall and finds some place to meditate until midnight. Sometimes a monk will enter such deep meditation that he loses all consciousness, not realizing the passing of time until the morning gong is heard. Such deep unconsciousness was once attained by a monk who unfortunately fell into the river from the rock on which he had been doing zazen. The next morning a fisherman found him floating in the river, pulled him out, and warmed him by the fire. He soon woke from unconsciousness, a state in which he had not swallowed even a drop of water. This story illustrates how deeply a man can meditate.

64. Kentan   The Master's Visit to the Meditation Hall

The Rōshi sometimes visits the meditation hall to survey the meditating monks. This is a formal ceremony in which the Master demonstrates his position as Master by scrutinizing the monks, and in which the monks show their sincerity and eagerness by a serious manner of meditating. For those who have experienced difficulty in improving the state of their minds, it is a very encouraging moment when the Master comes near them. The Rōshi at the same time verifies attendance, then returns to his room for general consultation.

65. Sōsan　　General Consultation with the Master

　　Immediately after the Rōshi's survey the monks attend his general consultation, a meeting which is more ceremonial than the private consultation (dokusan). At the latter, the order for consultation is determined by the order in which the monks arrive in the waiting room, each signaling his entrance by striking a small gong. In the general consultation, the order of entry is fixed according to the time each monk entered the monastery. The shika signals the entrance of each.

66. Enjudō   Healing Room

Whenever a monk becomes ill he may be consigned to the healing room, located near the meditation hall, to recover. The rules of this room are as follows:

> The man who uses this room must concentrate his whole being on his given kōan, even while ill in bed. He must not allow his mind to relax, but must keep training it; otherwise, his disease may become incurable. First, the prevention of fire is the most important concern. Second, wine and strong smelling foods are not permitted, even as medicine. Third, do not be careless about what is loaned to one. Fourth, reading, writing, and talking are not permitted. If one stays more than two nights, he must have a ceremony before returning to the meditation hall, as with initiates to the monastery.

67. Inji-gyō   Secret Good Deeds

The virtue gained through performing a secret deed is of special importance in the monastery. We notice immediately any one of outstanding virtue, even though we do not see him performing any virtuous deeds. The monks try to do good deeds in secret. Here, one is mending another's worn-out wooden clogs (geta); a second is taking down a friend's laundry before the rains come. Cleaning the toilet in the night is also considered a virtuous deed.

In China two monks were once traveling to visit a great Zen master. Upon finding a vegetable leaf floating downstream from the Master's hermitage, they decided to return home. Such a Master was obviously not a great man; he failed to practice the rule of wasting no living thing. Besides, as such a man would not perform secret deeds either, he certainly was no great Master.

除策

68. *Josaku*   Day of Relaxation

At certain times the monks are released from their
strict rules and allowed to enjoy various kinds of recreation, among
which sumō wrestling is popular.   In the monastic regimen, in
which the organization of life is strict, recreation is a welcome
relief, and an opportunity for obtaining mutual understanding
and comaraderie in the brotherhood.

半
斎

69. Hansai   Special Meal

On such days of relaxation the monks are served a special lunch. Though not allowed a luxurious meal even then, they are delighted to eat plenty of pure rice and good vegetables. Sometimes the monastery receives large amounts of money in order to serve the monks well on such occasions.

70. Katan　Participation in a General Zen Meeting

Every ten years or so there is a large meeting at the headquarters of certain Zen schools at which about two hundred monks gather from all over the country. There is a large zazen session and a lecture, but the most important event is the sanzen consultation carried on by forty Zen Masters. Each monk is given the opportunity to see a different Zen Master for improving his state of mind. Since each Master has his own unique characteristics in instruction, this meeting is a rare chance for a monk to learn from other monks and Masters outside his own monastery.

71. Kōjū-sai   Reception Day for Adherents

Once a year all the adherents are invited to the monastery, reversing the normal procedure in which monks are entertained in their homes. The Zen Master and monks chant scripture in the main hall for the adherents' ancestors; afterwards, the guests are served delicious Zen dishes prepared by the monks themselves. In the afternoon the guests are guided through the temple and have explained to them the spirit of Zen as expressed all through the monastery grounds.

更
衣

72. Kōe   Seasonal Change of Robes

On July first and October fifth the monks change robes
for the season ahead. Since each monk wears the same robe for
several months, it becomes very worn, and changing it gives him a
fresh, clean feeling. The worn robe is mended and put away in a
chest of drawers, an action indicating a definite passage of time
for the monk. The summer garment is made of flax, and the winter
one of cotton — fabrics considered simplest by the Japanese.

73. Hange   Midterm Day

On the day halfway through the rainy season, monks are served traditional rice cakes to celebrate their completing the half-term. About this time the weather changes from the comfortable rainy season to the hot days of summer, during which mosquitoes and humidity bring real discomfort to the monks as they meditate.

Looking through the lattice in the meditation hall, one can observe the changes in the seasons.

74. Kyōō   Special Meal of Noodles

The Japanese noodle (udon) is a very wholesome food to hungry monks. They may eat as much as they like, and they may suck them up noisily to cool them. Our poor friend unfortunately has no time to eat, as he must fan his brothers who are perspiring from the summer heat.

起
單
留
錫

75. Kitan ryūshaku   Term-end Examination

Each monk is called before the three highest monks at term's end for an examination, to determine whether or not he will be permitted to remain in the monastery. The monk writes down his desires about remaining in or leaving the monastery. If he wishes to remain, he is severely reproached for his behavior during the past term and must promise to endure the harsher training of the one to come.

76. Kōtai shitaku　Preparation for Rotation of Duties

As pickles are one of the main side dishes in the monastery, several tubs of them are kept in a small cottage within the grounds. (Compare illustration 86.) Radishes are usually pickled at the end of the year, and kept from eight months to sometimes two or three years. At the end of each term the monks must properly prepare the pickling equipment for those who will take over during the coming term. The strong smell of pickles becomes so agreeable that sometimes the cooks are filled with emotion upon having to conclude their task.

解
制

77. Kaisei   End of the Training Term

When the three months' retreat is completed, the monks celebrate their successful conclusion of this term by cooking a meal in the open. Broiling a fish is an example of their freedom from the strict Zen precepts, for the vegetarian diet is required throughout the year.

The man with the knife in one hand and a cat in the other is demonstrating a famous kōan: one day all the monks in the monastery of Master Nan-ch'uan (Nansen, 748-834) were quarreling over a cat. The Master picked up the cat and said, "If you say something, I will save her life. If you do not, I will kill her." As nobody could reply, the Master cut the cat in two. What would you have answered?

78. Niya sannichi   Two Nights' and Three Days' Absence

　　　Between the rainy and the snowy retreat periods there
are three months designated as the traveling term, during which
most monks today return to their home temples to aid in temple
maintenance. A few monks remain at the monastery to help
with its administrative details. They may, however, be absent
from the monastery for up to two nights and three days. This
monk is taking a nap on a hill in Nara, the oldest religious city in
Japan, famous for its tame deer. To monks who have been
isolated from the world for over three months, nature seems
very friendly.

棚
経

79. Tana-gyō   Honoring the Family Ancestors

In mid-August the Bon Festival is celebrated in Japan. Buddhists believe that during this time ancestral spirits return home. Each family, therefore, cleans its small house shrine to receive the ancestors, prepares meals for them and offers fruits, cakes, a burning candle, incense, and beautiful flowers. Monks are asked in to chant scripture in order to receive the ancestors respectfully. To show their appreciation, the housewives are busy entertaining the monks properly.

80. Segaki   Feeding the Hungry Spirits

During Obon, at the monastery as at ordinary temples, a wooden platform is built and placed on the veranda of the main hall. The monks chant scripture every evening in front of this platform; at the same time, they scatter healing water into the air to invite the hungry spirits (gaki). The flags around the platform indicate to the spirits where they should gather. On the fifteenth of August the Master and the monks perform a large segaki ceremony for the spirits, serving various kinds of food from the mountains, plains, and seas of Japan. Rice and water are scattered by laymen as well as by monastic participants in the ceremony. Even Zen monks engage in these aspects of popular Japanese religious life. This heritage has been important in helping to preserve the higher principles of Zen Buddhism in Japan.

彼岸鉢

81. Higan-hatsu   Begging Tour during the Equinox

The monks take long begging tours, especially during the weeks of the spring and fall equinoxes, and may walk as many as fifty miles in one day. When the monks walk in a line through a large city in which no Zen monastery exists, the city residents are greatly pleased and willingly donate to them. Such a long trip thus becomes an encouraging experience for both monks and laymen. These monks are in Ōsaka, one of Japan's largest cities, famous for its ancient castle.

82. Kyūsoku　Day of Rest

On the day following a begging tour, or after particularly hard labor, the monks are given a day of rest. They may spend this time doing whatever they like, but must remain within the monastery. Some continue their meditation, so other monks maintain silence as usual. The monks on the bench are enjoying some tea, while our friend is peeling a chestnut he found in the garden.

83. Daruma-ki   Memorial Day for Bodhidharma

The history of Zen Buddhism dates from the coming of Bodhidharma (Daruma) from India to China in A.D. 520. His teachings in China can be summarized as follows:

A special transmission outside the scriptures.

No dependence on words or letters.

Direct pointing at the soul of man.

Seeing into one's nature and the attainment of Buddhahood.

Zen Buddhism celebrates this memorial day on October 5. The image of Bodhidharma can be found all over Japan, especially as a toy for children, like the one our friend is holding.

開山忌

84. *Kaisan-ki* *Memorial Day for the Founder of the Monastery*

Each monastery celebrates a great Zen Master as its founder. Founder's memorial day is among the monastery's important celebrations to which all former monks are invited. The old priests have come from their local temples to donate money as a way of encouraging the monks and of maintaining the monastery. Note the lacquered bowls, indicative of a special occasion.

85. Daikon-hatsu Collecting Radishes

At the end of October the monks leave the monastery and go into the countryside to ask for the large, white radishes that are later used for pickling. Each year the farmers expect the monks and prepare a sufficient number of dried radishes for them. It is this type of support which, in fact, makes the monastic life possible and the monks feel a great indebtedness for the goodwill of these laymen.

漬
物

86. Tsukemono   Making Pickles

　　Once collected, the radishes are quickly pickled and stored in a dark cottage until the next summer. (Compare illustration 76.) Because they have been dried previously by the farmers, the radishes may be immediately pickled in large tubs with rice bran and salt. Sometimes seaweed or the dried skins of persimmons are added to make the pickles more delicious.

87. Rōhatsu — Training Week Commemorating the Buddha's Enlightenment

From the first to the morning of the eighth of December the monks engage in the strictest meditation of the year in memory of the Buddha's experience of satori more than twenty-five centuries ago. Through these seven days the monks rarely leave their meditating posture, even to lie down, just like monks of past centuries. All meals are brought to the meditation hall so that the monks there may dedicate this entire period to zazen. The activities of the week consist entirely of meditation and the Master's discourses, except that at midnight the monks may take a two-hour nap, but during which they must not lie down. Snow often blows into the meditation hall through the windows, and when a fire is built, the silence of the meditating monks gives way to the sound of crackling wood. Illustrated is a moment of relaxation outside the meditation hall.

88. Tōya   Night of the Winter Solstice

Once a year, on the night of the winter solstice, the monks enjoy a party. All come together to sing, dance, drink, and perform stunts. Even the Master participates so that the other monks may become closer to him who, on this occasion, is perhaps reminded of his own youth. On this night, the Master and the monks are on the same plane — as human beings. The lay adherents of the monastery provide wine and food for this occasion and may also enjoy the company of the monks, some of whom may in future become great Zen leaders.

正月支度

89. *Shōgatsu shitaku*　Preparations for the New Year

　　At the end of the year, as is customary in Japan, the monks
prepare a large number of rice cakes. The work is divided into
separate tasks such as steaming the rice, pounding it when
steamed, and making the round cakes. Because the process
requires special skills, it is impressive to see.

90. Zuii-za   Sitting at Ease

Three days of rest are allowed over the New Year's period. The decoration on the boxes on the ledge in the background is typical for this season. The two rice cakes are topped with a mandarin orange, and these in turn are put into the boxes over a white bean leaf on white paper. The monks on the left are playing go, one of Japan's favorite games. The monk on the right is napping in formal position.

大般若

91. Dai-hannya   Reading the Sutra Titles

During the first three days of the New Year the monks
read the titles of the six hundred volumes of the *Prajñāpāramitā
Sutra (Hannya-haramitsu-kyō)* in a loud voice, turning the volumes
around three times to the right and three times to the left while
doing so. These are some of the central texts in Mahāyāna
Buddhism, and it is widely believed that merely to turn them
around in this manner provides as much merit as if one had read
them through. This is not an unimportant consideration, since
Buddhism has more than five thousand volumes of scripture.

見
性

92. Kenshō   Experiencing Awareness

    The wonderful moment of satori is expressed vividly
here; no further comment is called for. Our friend is now in the
hand of the Buddha. Each person must experience this for
himself, at least once in his life.

93. Kōtai   Rotation of Major Duties

At the end of January the monks exchange their basic tasks in the monastic life. Those who have been staying in the meditation hall now move to the administrative quarters; those who have been managing the affairs of the monastery in the administrative quarters now devote themselves entirely to zazen. The monks feel regret at leaving friends they have worked with during the past term, since they help one another in all these activities.

暫
暇

94. Zanka   Returning to the Home Temple

Our friend has now returned to his home temple, where the neighbors and adherents welcome him at the gate, bringing wine and fish to show their gratitude for his return, and to congratulate him upon the completion of his monastic life. The people are happy to have such a well-trained successor priest in the temple and do all they can to show their joy. Notice how much our friend's face has changed since we saw him leaving the temple for the monastery.

95. Hinsetsu   Receiving Visitors at the Head Temple

The artist included two extra drawings after completing
the original set. This one shows part of the large compound of the
head temple of the monastery to which he belonged, Tōfukuji in
Kyōto, especially famous for its huge buildings. This one is the
old meditation hall where at least two hundred monks once lived
together, though today it is kept as a national treasure and is
not used. Looking inside, we can visualize the generations of
discipline practiced upon the meditation platform.

96. HŌKŌ   Escapade at Night

A very informal, yet dear secret of the Zen priest from his youthful days in the monastery is the nightly escape over the monastery wall to relax and drink in town. The artist did not hesitate to draw this from his own youthful recollections.

Many years ago in Japan at the monastery of the great Zen Master Sengai (1750-1837), one monk climbed over the mud wall every night to go into town. The Master knew this, and one evening meditated at the designated spot after having removed the stone the monk ordinarily used for jumping over the wall. In the early dawn the monk returned to the monastery and jumped onto the head of the Master, without realizing what he had done until later when told that the Master was suffering from a severe headache. The monk's regret for this deed led him on to become a great Zen Master later in life. Such a humorous story is a beautiful way of understanding the real humanity of the Zen brothers and the method of training in Zen.

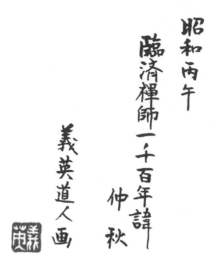

97. Artist's Signature

The inscription reads: "The middle of autumn, 1966, drawn by Giei Satō in celebration of the eleven hundredth anniversary of Lin-chi (Rinzai), the Ch'an forerunner of Rinzai Zen Buddhism."

Dave Comstock

Tōfukuji

Tōfukuji is the head temple of the Tōfukuji school of the Rinzai sect of Zen Buddhism. It was built in 1236 on the instructions of Fujiwara Michiie, the great statesman of the Heian period, who desired to build in Kyōto a temple comparable to Tōdaiji and Kōfukuji, the great temple complexes in Nara. Even its name, Tōfukuji, is a combination of one character from the names of each of these Nara temples. Its original buildings were burned, but were rebuilt in the 15th c. according to the original plans. About this time it flourished as one of the Five Great Temples of Kyōto. Its many compounds and subtemples survived the ravages of war and fire until the late Meiji period when the Butsudō (Buddha hall) and the

Hodō (lecture hall) were burned. However, it even now retains the magnificent scale characteristic of a medieval Zen temple.

The Sanmon gate, a National Treasure, is the oldest Zen main gate in Japan. The Zendō (meditation hall), Tesu (lavatory), and Yokushitsu (bathing room) are also survivals from the early Muromachi period (14th century). The Hondō (main hall) and the Hōjō (head priest's quarters) are recent reconstructions. The valley up to the Kaisandō, spanned by its three bridges, is famous for its maple leaves in autumn.

Kyōto City

The above is from an official sign erected outside the Tōfukuji by the city of Kyōto. The syllable *ji* in these names means "temple"; Tōfukuji is therefore Tōfuku Temple, and so on.

Appendix

Rules Regulating the Daily Life

The most urgent task is to study and master Zen. Therefore, whenever you have a view to discuss with the master, consult with the directing monk (jikijitsu) and try to see the master regardless of the hours of the day.

1. When entering the Zendo, fold your hands, palm to palm, before your chest; when going out of it, hold your hands, the right over the left, in front of the chest. Let your walking and standing be duly decorous. Do not walk across the front of the Mañjuśrī shrine; be not in a flurry or swaggering when walking the floor.

2. During the meditation hours, no one is permitted to leave the Hall except for interviewing the master. To other necessary movements, the intermission hours are to be devoted. While outside, no whispering, no tarrying is allowed.

3. When the kinhin (walking) goes on, do not remain in your seats; when walking do not shuffle your sandals. If you are, on account of disease, prevented from taking part in the kinhin, with the consent of the directing monk (jikijitsu) stand on the floor at your seat.

4. The keisaku (warning-stick) is to be used with discrimination on the monks, whether they are dozing or not. When submitting to the warning stick, courteously fold your hands and bow; do not permit any egoistic thoughts to assert themselves and cherish anger.

5. At the time of tea-ceremony (sarei) taking place twice a day, no one shall be absent; no left-overs are to be thrown on the floor.

6. No sundry articles are to be scattered about your seats (tan).

Reprinted from Daisetz Teitaro Suzuki, The Training of the Zen Buddhist Monk (New York: University Books, 1965) by permission of Lyle Stuart, Inc.

No writing materials are allowed. Do not take off your upper garment at your seats when going out of the back door.

7. *Even when the Zendo is not in regular session, you are not to pass your time dozing, sitting against the back wall.*

8. *No one is allowed on his own accord to use the warning-stick (keisaku) although he may be suffering from the stiffness of his shoulder-muscles.*

9. *Going out to town or visiting the jōjū quarters is not permitted: if absolutely necessary, transact the business through the attendants (jisha) of the Zendo; otherwise, all private affairs are to be settled on the "needle and moxa" days (hashin kyūji).*

10. *On ordinary days the monks are not allowed at the attendants' quarters (jisharyo); if necessary, the jikijitsu (directing monk) is to be notified.*

11. *At the time of morning service, the dozing ones are to be severely dealt with the keisaku (warning-stick).*

12. *At meal-time the monks are to conduct themselves quietly and to make no noise in the handling of the bowls; the waiting monks should move about quietly and in due decorum.*

13. *When the meditation hours are over at night, go right to bed; do not disturb others by sutra-reading, or bowings, or whispering with the neighbouring monks.*

14. *During the term, the monks are not allowed to leave the monastery unless their teachers or parents are critically ill or dead.*

15. *When a monk is newly admitted into the Brotherhood, the fact is announced and he takes the seat assigned to him; but before this is done, he must first make bows to the Holy Monk (i.e., Mañjuśrī), and then pay his respect to the head of the tan and to the jikijitsu (directing monk).*

16. *When the monks go out for their begging round, they are not to swing their arms, or put their hands inside the dress, or walk the*

streets staggeringly, or whisper to one another; for such behaviours are damaging to the dignity of monkhood. If they meet horses, carriages, etc., in the streets, be careful to avoid walking against them. In all their movements, the monks ought to be orderly.

17. The days bearing the numbers four and nine, are the days for general sweeping, shaving, bathing, working outdoors, etc.; sewing, moxa-burning, etc. may also take place on these days. The monks are then not supposed to visit one another and pass their time in talking idly, cracking jokes, and laughing nonsensically.

18. As to fixing bath days for the Brotherhood, the monks entrusted with the task are requested to consult the shikaryo (head of the general office) and act according to his directions.

19. When any one is indisposed, the matter is to be reported to the jikijitsu and the attendant-monk (jisha), and the sick one will be removed from the Zendo. While being nursed, he is neither to read books, nor to be engaged in literary work, nor to pass his time in idle talk. If he comes back after five days, he is expected to perform the rite of "returning to the Zendo."

The above regulations are to be carefully taken notice of. Those who violate belong to the family of the Evil One and interfere with the welfare of the community. They are to be expelled speedily after holding a council. The reason is to preserve as long as possible the life of the community.

Regulations of the Sick-room

Anyone who happens to be the occupant of this room because of ill health, is not to forget practising zazen silently along with taking medicine, even with his head on the pillow. Never neglect exercising himself in the cultivation of the right thought. When this is not done, the disease may be aggravated and the medicine cease to be effective. Three doses of medicine are to be taken daily; each basketful of charcoal costs three sen.

1. Fire of all kind is to be carefully kept under control.

2. Neither saké nor herbs of the onion family are allowed even as medicine. According to the nature of the disease, special cooking is allowed after reporting to the office. Other things are prohibited.

3. Be careful not to soil the bedding, etc.

4. While in sick-bed, a monk is not allowed to read books, to engage in literary work, or to idle away his time in trivial talk. If he comes out of the sick-room after staying away for five days, he is expected to perform the rite of "returning to the Zendo."

Regulations of the Official Quarters (Jyōjū)

The most essential business of monkhood is to study Zen, and you are expected to exert yourselves in this. After the daily work, keep your evening meditation as in the Zendo. Says an ancient master, "The exercise while working is hundreds of thousands of times more valuable than the one practised while in quietude." Keeping this in mind, exert yourselves to the best of your abilities.

1. Take the best care of all kinds of fire and light.

2. At the morning and the evening service and on other occasions requiring attendance, the monk-officials are not to fall behind the others.

3. At meal-times try by all means to attend a second sitting if you are detained by your work. In handling the bowls, in sipping soup, you are not to make a noise. The waiting-monks must behave orderly and with decorum.

4. In going the begging rounds or in performing outdoor work, you are also expected to join the others; if you are prevented from this, do not neglect reporting the fact at the shikaryo.

5. Do not visit other official rooms and spend the time in gossipping and talking trivialities whereby interrupting their hours of meditation.

When business requires visits, do not prolong them beyond absolute necessity.

6. Going out in town is strictly forbidden. If it is necessary to go out of the gate, the shikaryo is to be notified. When out in town the mannerly behavior of monkhood is expected.

7. When sick and not able to attend the service, etc, the fact is to be reported at the shikaryo; such monks are not to visit other official rooms.

8. When the evening meditation hours are over, each monk is to retire at once to his own bed. No wastage of the light is allowed by sitting up late and talking nonsense. The bedding and other articles are to be kept clean.

9. All the articles and pieces of furniture belonging to the jyōjū quarters are to be used with the utmost care. After use, take note to return them where they are kept. Says an ancient master: "All the belongings of the jyōjū are to be used as a man does his own eyes."

10. The sandals are not to be left carelessly on the floor. While stepping up and down the hall, do not make rustling sounds. Do not make light of the trivial deeds of daily life, for great virtues are born of them. Pray, be mindful of all that has been stated above.

Regulations of the Lodging Room

Monks intently bent on the mastery of Zen go on a pilgrimage in search of an able master and superior friends. When the evening comes, they find out a monastery where they may pass the night. Being permitted to the lodging room, they release themselves of the travelling outfit, and sit in the meditation posture facing the wall. It is to be most regretted that recently there are some travelling monks who have no desire to conduct themselves in accordance with old usage. The main point for the monks, however, is to devote their entire energy to the settlement of the gravest business they can have in this life in whatever surroundings they may find themselves. The meaning of the pilgrimage in Zen lies nowhere else but here, as was anciently seen in the company of Seppo, Ganto, and Kinzan. O monks, be ever diligent!

1. After the evening bell is struck, no travelling monks are admitted.

2. Do not ask for a second night's lodging however stormy and windy the day may be. In case of sickness this rule is waived.

3. No dozing against the travelling bag is allowed. The lodging monk is not to go to bed until the evening meditation hours are over or until a notice to that effect is given to him.

4. Attend the morning service when the bell in the Hall is heard; the kesa may be omitted.

5. The morning gruel is served when the umpan ("cloud-board") is struck.

6. No light is to be burned in the night.

Regulations of the Bath-room

While taking a bath, the "exquisite touch" of warmth must be made to lead to the "realization of the nature of water." No idle talking is allowed here. Before and after the bath, proper respect is to be paid to the venerable Bhadra.

1. The best care must be taken of fire.

2. The bath-room work is attended in turn by the monks from the Zendo. Otherwise, orders are issued from the shikaryo.

3. When the master takes his bath, have his attendants notified. In case of other respectable personages, special attention will be given to the cleanliness and orderliness of the bath-room.

4. When the bath is ready, the wooden blocks are clapped according to the regulations, and the monks led in rotation to the room by the Zendo attendants.

5. For the fuel, dead leaves gathered from the woods and other waste materials are to be used.

6. When the bathing is all over, be thorough in scraping all the embers and hot ashes out from under the bathing pot and have them completely extinguished.

7. On the day following, the bath-tub will be thoroughly scrubbed, and the entire room nicely cleansed, while the vessels are properly arranged.

The above articles are to be observed at all points. No random use of the bath-room is permitted, which may interrupt the speedy execution of the public office.

Glossary

The Japanese words listed here in romanized transliteration are followed by their Sino-Japanese characters (kanji) and by the number of the commentary in which they occur. A number in color indicates that the word appears in the title of a commentary, and thus provides a partial index to the illustrations by topic. Literal translations, given for some words, are enclosed in quotation marks.

Most words defined or explained upon their first appearance in the text are not defined here. Words in unabridged (American) English dictionaries are not in color or italics in the text and are not listed here.

angya 行脚 2, "going on foot": a Buddhist pilgrimage.

antan 安單 9.

baitō 梅糖 16, "plum sugar."

banka 晩課 37, 38.

banka sōji 晩課 掃除 38.

Bon 盆 79, 80. Usually called Obon; in full, Urabon, from Skt. Ullambana.

Busshin-gyō 仏心行 58, "Buddha-mind act.."

Butsuden 仏殿 34. Temple building enshrining an image or images of the Buddha; also, Butsudō or hondō.

chōka 朝課 15.

daidō mumon 大道無門 3. From the preface to the Mumonkan, a Zen text by Hui-k'ai (1183-1260), a monk of the later Sung dynasty. Discourses on the text, comprising forty-eight cases, are frequently held in Zen monasteries.

Dai-hannya 大般若 91, "Great Prajñā": a ceremony honoring the *Prajñāpāramitā* (Japanese: *Hannya-haramitsu*) Sutra. Also, *Hannya-e*.

daikon-hatsu 大根鉢 85.

Daruma 達磨 83. Japanese name for Bodhidharma.

Daruma-ki 達磨忌 83.

deshi 弟子 2. A disciple or pupil of a *shishō*.

dokusan 独参 22. Individual consultation with a Zen Master; a form of *sanzen*.

dōnai 堂内 16. That part of a monastery in which the monks live, meditate, worship, etc., as opposed to the administrative quarters (*jōjū*).

dōnai fugin 堂内諷経 16.

enju 園頭 30.

enjudō 延寿堂 66, "life-prolonging room": the healing room of the monastery.

fugin 諷経 16, 17, "chanting scriptures."

fūsu 副司 42. The monk in charge of the monastery's accounts and business affairs.

fuzui 附随 17, 45. A monk assigned as an attendant to the head monk.

gaki 餓鬼 80.

Gyōdō 行道 35. Reading scripture in movement.

handaikan 飯台看 19.

hange 半夏 73.

hansai 半斎 69.

hashin kyūji 把針灸治 46, "taking up the needle and moxa treatment."

higan-hatsu 彼岸鉢 81. From *higan* "equinox" and *hatsu* "bowl," used as a suffix for various types of begging — *takuhatsu*, *higan-hatsu*, etc.

hinsetsu 賓接 95.

hokku 法鼓 60.

hōkō 放行 96.

hondō 本堂 14, "main hall": another term for the Butsuden or Buddha hall.

hō...u 法雨 25.

inji 隠侍 17. Attendant, see sannō.

inji-gyō 隠事行 67.

jihatsu 持鉢 2. The bowl used by a monk for meals and begging.

jikijitsu 直日 16, 54. The elder monk who supervises the others during meditation, worship, etc.

jōjū 常住 17. The administrative quarters of a monastery; such as offices, kitchen, etc.; cf. dōnai.

jōjū fugin 常住諷経 17.

josaku 除策 68. A day or period of relaxation from monastery routine.

kaichin 解定 41, "release from the samadhi meditation": retiring at night.

kaihan 開板 11, "opening the han": the thrice-daily announcement of time.

kaijō 開静 13, "opening the samadhi meditation": arising in the morning.

kaikō 開講 51.

kaisan-ki 開山忌 84.

kaisei 解制 77.

kaiyoku 開浴 33, "opening the bath": bathing.

kanshō 喚鐘 56.

kashaku 掛錫 3, "hanging up the priest's staff."

katan 加担 70.

kayu 粥 18.

keisaku 警策 54, 55. The staff or stick used to administer discipline during meditation.

kenshō 見性 92, "seeing one's nature": another term for satori.

kentan 検単　64, "inspecting the platform."

kiin 帰院　27.

kikan 亀鑑　49.

kiku 規矩　12.

kinhin 経行　59, "Sutra-going": the practice of meditation while walking in the meditation hall.

kitan ryūshaku 起単留錫　75.

kōe 更衣　72.

kōjū-sai 講中斎　71.

kokuhō 告報　50.

konshō 昏鐘　39.

kōtai 交代　76, 93. Exchange or rotation of duties. See *shitaku.*

kufū 工夫　62. A device, means, expedient: here, a potential means of achieving *satori.*

kyōō 饗応　74. A treat or special meal.

kyūsoku 休息　82.

Mañjuśrī, see Monju Bosatsu.

miso 味噌 28, bean paste.

mogusa 艾　46. A plant (also called *yomogi*), a pinch of whose dried, crushed leaves are placed in contact with the skin and ignited. This traditional medical treatment is referred to as moxacautery (*kyūji*).

Monju Bosatsu 文珠菩薩　8, 16. Japanese name for *Mañjuśrī.*

Mumonkan 無門関　3, 29. An important collection of 48 *kōan* compiled in China during the thirteenth century.

nikki 日記　1. Diary, journal.

nisshitsu 入室　57.

nitten sōji 日典掃除　23, "daily cleaning."

niwa-zume 庭詰　4, 6, "occupying the courtyard": an examination undergone by a supplicant prior to his admission to the monastery.

niya sannichi 二夜三日　78.

Obon, see *Bon.*

ō-shikunichi 大四九日 *32,* "*great shikunichi*": *a twice-monthly day of rest for the monks.*

Rōhatsu 臘八 *87,* "*the eighth day of the twelfth lunar month.*"

Rōshi 老師 , "*old teacher*": *a Zen Master.*

saba 生飯 *19.*

saiza 斎座 *28.*

samu 作務 *29.*

sandō 参道 *8,* "*proceeding to the hall.*"

sannō 三応 *17, 43.*

sanzen 参禅 *22, 70. To go to a Zen Master to receive instruction, usually through the use of the kōan.*

sarei 茶礼 *21, 47. Daily tea ceremony. See also shuttō.*

segaki 施餓鬼 *80,* "*feeding the gaki.*"

sembutsu-jō 選仏場 *8.*

sesshin 接心 *52, 54. A semiannual week of intensive meditation and special lectures.*

shijō 止静 *54.*

shika 知客 *7, 20, 45, 65. The head monk or chief administrator of a Zen monastery; shikaryo* 知客察 *, his quarters.*

shikunichi 四九日 *31, 32,* "*four-nine days.*"

shishō 師匠 *2. A master or teacher in religion, art, scholarship, etc., a kind of spiritual father to his deshi or disciples.*

shitaku 支度 *76, 89,* "*preparations.*"

shōgatsu shitaku 正月支度 *89.*

shōkei 小憩 *26.*

shōken 相見 *10,* "*mutual seeing*": *the first meeting of novice and Rōshi.*

shukushin 祝聖 *34.*

shukuza 粥座 *20.*

shūmai 集米 *24,* "*gathering rice.*"

shussai 出斎 44.

shuttō 出頭 14, 47. To enter or put in an appearance, as in sarei shuttō.

shuya 守夜 40.

sōdō 僧堂 2, "priest (monk) hall": a Zen monastery.

sōji 掃除 23, 38. Cleaning, housecleaning.

sōsan 総参 65. General consultation with a Zen Master; a form of sanzen. Cf. dokusan.

sōzarei 総茶礼 21, 48. "general tea-ceremony": cf. sarei.

takuhatsu 托鉢 25, "carrying the bowl": the practice of begging by monks.

tan 単 8, "platform," seat.

tana-gyō 棚経 79.

tanga 旦過 5. See tanga-ryō.

tanga-ryō 旦過寮 5. Room set aside for overnight lodging (tanga) of itinerant priests or novices desiring to enter the monastery.

tanga-zume 旦過詰 6, "occupying the tanga": cf. niwa-zume.

teihatsu 剃髪 31.

teishō 提唱 51, 61. Discourse by a Rōshi upon a Zen text.

tenjin 点心 36.

tenzo 典座 17, 18.

tōya 冬夜 88.

tsukemono 漬物 86. Japanese pickled vegetables.

yaza 夜坐 63.

zanka 暫暇 94.

zazen 坐禅 12, 16, 53, 63, 70, 87, 93. Meditation in a prescribed, cross-legged posture in Zen Buddhism.

zendō 禅堂 2, 8, 30, "meditation hall": building in which monks live and practice zazen. Also used in a broader sense to refer to a Zen monastery as a whole.

Zen-shū 禅宗 The Zen sect of Buddhism.

zuii-za 随意坐 90, "sitting as one pleases." Release from daily rule.